Your Child's Emotional Health: Adolescence

Philadelphia Child Guidance Center

Your Child's Emotional Health: Adolescence

PHILADELPHIA CHILD GUIDANCE CENTER WITH JACK MAGUIRE

Produced by The Philip Lief Group, Inc.

Macmillan • USA

This book is not intended as a substitute for the professional advice of a doctor or mental health professional. The reader should regularly consult a physician or appropriate health care practitioner in matters relating to health, particularly with respect to any symptoms that may require diagnosis or medical attention.

MACMILLAN
A Prentice Hall Macmillan Company
15 Columbus Circle
New York, NY 10023

Published by arrangement with   The Philip Lief Group, Inc.
                                6 West 20th Street
                                New York, NY 10011

MACMILLAN is a registered trademark of Macmillan, Inc.

Library of Congress Cataloging-in-Publication Data

Your child's emotional health. Adolescence / Philadelphia Child
  Guidance Center with Jack Maguire.
      p.   cm.
  Includes index.
  ISBN 0-02-860003-7
  1. Emotions in adolescence.   2. Emotional problems of children.
I. Maguire, Jack.   II. Philadelphia Child Guidance Center.
BF724.3.E5Y675   1995
649'.125—dc20   94-34153
                                                             CIP

Manufactured in the United States of America

10   9   8   7   6   5   4   3   2   1

This book is dedicated to Margie Ouellette
and to her children,
Amanda, Carly, and Brittany.
I am proud to be a part of their family.

Contents

Preface

Children seldom say that they need help. More often their behaviors tell us that they do. They may suffer vague, slowly evolving difficulties at home, at school, or with their peers. Or they may exhibit sudden, marked changes in their conduct and mood that pervade every aspect of their lives.

Each year, thousands of children, adolescents, and their families get help from Philadelphia Child Guidance Center (PCGC). As one of the foremost centers in the country for child and adolescent psychiatric care, PCGC offers services that are specialized and individually designed to meet the needs of each child and family. Often working in closely cooperative teams, staff members help families recognize, expand, and mobilize their strengths to make life more fulfilling for the affected child as well as for the family as a whole.

Since PCGC's origin in 1925 as one of the first centers in the world devoted to child psychiatry, it has enjoyed an international reputation for its excellent treatment and innovative research. The founding director, Frederick H. Allen, M.D., was the first board-certified child psychiatrist in the United States as well as one of the first psychiatrists to address the problems of the child in the context of the family. Within his historic thirty-year tenure, PCGC achieved a leadership position in the study and treatment of emotional problems affecting children from birth through adolescence.

Later, under the auspices of Director Salvador Minuchin, M.D., PCGC pioneered the development of structural family therapy, a systems-oriented approach that views diagnosis and treatment of a child in the context of the family and social relationships in which she or he lives. Included in that context are the child's extended family, friends, caretakers, school, and all agencies in the culture at large—social, legal, religious, recreational, and health oriented—that influence the child's life.

Today, under the clinical direction of Alberto C. Serrano, M.D., PCGC's staff of 230 professionals provides a broad range of diagnostic and therapeutic programs that directly benefit the mid-Atlantic region of the United States and serve as models for other diagnostic and therapeutic programs throughout the nation and abroad. Thanks to its strong affiliation with the University of Pennsylvania Medical School, The Children's Hospital of Philadelphia, and Children's Seashore House, PCGC is a major component of one of the most advanced health-care and health-care research centers in the country.

This books draws upon the unique experience and expertise of PCGC to offer you, as parents, practical guidelines for raising your child to be emotionally healthy. Specifically, it helps you perform the following, especially challenging activities:

■ identify and assess your child's emotional states, problems, capabilities, and needs;

■ develop an effective parenting style that best suits you and your child as individuals;

■ address the most common and most troublesome emotional difficulties that can arise in the course of your child's life;

■ ensure the emotional well-being of all family members during any emotional crisis experienced by your family as a whole or by your child individually;

■ determine if and when you, your family, and your child need professional help in managing emotional difficulties;

■ secure the professional help that is most appropriate for you, your family, and your child, according to the situation at hand.

Love for a child comes naturally to a parent and can go far toward giving a child emotional security. Parenting skills, however, are also required to meet a child's emotional needs, and they do *not* come naturally. Instead, parents must learn them.

This book is specially designed to help parents help themselves so that they in turn can help their children. Underlying everything that PCGC does—and represents—is the belief that family members have the ability to work together to solve their problems and that each family member can achieve a new and more rewarding life in the process.

Acknowledgments

Among the many people outside Philadelphia Child Guidance Center who were helpful in putting this book together, I'd like to give special thanks to Eva Weiss, to The Philip Lief Group as a whole, and to Natalie Chapman, my editor at Macmillan. Their "writer guidance" was invaluable.

Your Child's Emotional Health: Adolescence

Introduction

L ife during adolescence is rife with paradoxes. The word *adolescence* itself means "to be in the process of becoming adult," which signifies that a teenager has no fixed characteristics or identity. Instead, she or he is a transitional being, a changeling, who progresses through various and unpredictably shifting degrees of being part child, part adult, and part in-between. Although studies indicate that most teenagers are not *seriously* troubled despite popular opinion that they are, the potential for emotional turbulence is ever-present.

One major paradox of adolescence involves the nature of a teenager's emotional dependence on her or his parents. While typical, self-absorbed adolescents are always craving personal freedom from their parents, they still want—and need—their love just as much as ever.

All too easily teenagers can feel as if they are no longer cute, little, helpless, or even innocent enough to attract such love. And all too easily parents assume that their teenage children don't like to be "babied" with the same old expressions of love. This latter assumption may or may not be true; but in either case, the sad result is that many parents become inhibited about expressing their love to their teenage children in *any* direct manner, which only makes their children feel all the more unloved.

Another major paradox of adolescence has to do with the powerful conflict between rationality and irrationality in the teenage psyche. For long periods of time during a child's adolescence, it can appear as if two equally strong internal forces—order and chaos—are wrestling for control of all words and actions, with neither force very often winning a decisive victory.

On the "order" side, teenagers are intensely concerned with understanding *why* things are as they are, from the way society in general operates to the way their parents run their particular household. They'll argue social and family policies fiercely and doggedly, with an apparent reverence for logic, reason, and clarity that can often make them appear far more mature and judicious than they really are.

On the "chaos" side, teenagers are predisposed to experiment more creatively from time to time with their emerging adulthood, testing the limits of the pleasures and pains that it has to offer. On many occasions, this tendency can lead to an impulsive disregard of reason, rules, or responsibilities for the sake of establishing and feeling one's own individuality. Sometimes this tendency can lead even further toward a deliberate and outright defiance of what is right or logical— perhaps even a reckless act of thrill seeking that may end in disaster.

Yet another major paradox of adolescence involves the *rate* at which teenagers evolve from being immature children into being mature adults. This rate varies not only *among* individual teenagers in a group but also *within* each individual teenager, according to which particular aspects of his or her life are under consideration.

In some respects, a teenager can appear to grow up very fast, especially one in today's world. Within a few short years after puberty, most contemporary adolescent boys and girls are copying adult dress and behaviors fairly successfully, carrying on active sex lives, and earning enough money to buy themselves a significant amount of financial independence, at least as far as their day-to-day personal and social activities are concerned.

In other respects, today's teenagers are postponing their final coming of age further and further into the future, prolonging residence at home and/or overall dependence on their parents until after they have earned a college degree, achieved job security, or found someone with whom to start a family, or a life, of their own. Indeed, it's not at all uncommon today for individuals to remain emotionally dependent or "childlike" in their relationship with their parents until well into their twenties and even thirties.

In trying to work through these paradoxes to raise your adolescent child more effectively, here are some essential points to remember:

1. During your child's adolescence, you should expect and accept a certain rise in the number of emotional difficulties.

In the case of most children, the so-called middle years between age six and puberty are less emotionally turbulent for parent and child alike than the early years between birth and age six. Regrettably, this trend doesn't usually continue beyond the middle years into adolescence. Instead, the onset of adolescence, with its dramatic physical and social changes, initiates a return of sorts to the stormier emotional climate associated with the early years of childhood.

During turbulent adolescence, your perfectly "normal" child may do many things that will make you feel worried, ashamed, fearful, helpless, angry, or guilty. Here's just a sampling of various types of "normal" teenage problems that have distressing emotional causes and effects:

■ spending most of the time at home, silent and withdrawn;

■ driving a car around without a license;

■ treating adults in general with distrust and disrespect;

■ stealing money from wallets and private stashes;

■ attacking, quarreling with, and rejecting parents on very personal grounds, especially the "same sex" parent;

■ lying about activities and whereabouts;

■ defying household rules and family standards of decency;

■ staying out all night, whereabouts unknown;

■ shoplifting;

■ refusing to go anywhere with the family;

■ abusing drugs;

■ skipping school for extended periods of time;

■ running away;

■ tormenting younger children;

■ engaging in promiscuous sex.

Clearly some of these problems are more alarming than others, at least on the surface. Nevertheless, *all* of them are common among teenagers—regardless of sex, race, family status, moral upbringing, socioeconomic class, or geographic area. And although a child's emotional and behavioral history before becoming a teenager will have a strong impact on how she or he progresses through adolescence, so will all the new physical, social, and emotional challenges that are unique to adolescence and, to a great degree, unpredictable.

Because of these facts, no parent of a teenager can afford to dismiss any one of the above-mentioned problems as "inconceivable" or "intolerable" in the case of her or his child. Instead, every parent of a teenager must be somewhat prepared in advance to handle all of these problems so that she or he won't be completely at a loss if any one of them—or more—should arise.

When you, as a parent, are faced with such concerns, the key to maintaining your authority and sanity is to put each difficult situation involving your teenage child into its proper perspective. Accept what you can afford to accept—for your own sake, your child's sake, and your family's sake—whenever it's possible to do so. Reserve serious criticisms, disciplinary actions, or rescue attempts for situations that truly warrant them, based on your own informed and practical judgment.

2. *Your teenage child depends on you to be emotionally calm, steady, and strong*.

With so many emotional ups and downs and twists and turns going on in their lives, teenagers appreciate getting a sense of proportion from their parents, whether they openly acknowledge it or not. But such a sense is only one of the things teenagers are seeking from their parents.

Observing how any adult—but especially a parent—maintains a strong, emotionally secure center through good times and bad actually inspires teenagers to try to do the same thing themselves. By consciously and/or unconsciously imitating such models of mature steadiness, teenagers develop a more consistent, responsible, and balanced feeling for who they are and how they're getting along in life.

As the parent of a teenager, try to remain as composed and consistent as possible in your parenting style, particularly during difficult parent-child encounters. Don't let conversational negotiations degenerate into heated arguments. Above all, guard against taking out your personal anxieties and frustrations on your child by doing unto your child the same types of upsetting things that she or he does unto you.

3. *Throughout your child's adolescence, you should work together toward achieving a more mature and mutually independent parent-child relationship*.

Often parents of a teenager suffer consciously or subconsciously from a reluctance to yield *any* of their parental authority. They fear not only that their child might founder if they begin withdrawing their support and control but also that they might thereby start losing their child altogether.

In fact, an adolescent child's growth as an emotionally healthy and independent human being depends on a gradual giving up of parental authority so that the child can eventually manage and assume full responsibility for her or his own life and activities. In this process, parents don't *lose* their children. Instead, they let their children *loose* so that they can be free to form more mature and mutually rewarding relationships with everyone in their lives, including their parents.

As the parent of a teenage child, you need to appreciate these facts and use them as the basis for developing a flexible and less authoritarian parenting style. It's for your own good as well as that of your child.

Be alert for opportunities to trust your teenage child with new freedoms and responsibilities. Share with your child new, more adult-oriented interests and activities, as appropriate. Allow your child to experiment with new, less child-oriented ways of interacting or socializing with you in particular and with the family in general. And help your child lay the groundwork, block by block, for a new, satisfying, and self-reliant future life apart from you and the family.

4. *Your child never outgrows the need for your love, care, and respect*.

Although children may demand and deserve an increasing amount of independence from direct parental supervision and control as they progress through their teenage years, they will always need their parents to love them, to be concerned about their welfare, and to hold them in high regard. From these parental gifts they derive a great deal of their ongoing emotional security and sense of self-worth.

Always make sure that your teenage child realizes your love, care, and respect for her or him regardless of what she or he may do. In criticizing or disciplining your teenage child, be careful to focus your disapproval on the offending *act*, not on your *child* her- or himself. And occasionally go out of your way to express positive feelings about your child in ways that are appropriate to her or his current age and sensibilities.

This book offers guidelines that assist you in helping your child enjoy the pleasures and endure the pain that commonly accompanies adolescence. It is organized as follows:

1. SEXUALITY *(page 12)*

■ what to expect in terms of sexual activity during adolescence

■ how to help a teenage child be sexually safe and responsible

■ how to deal with problems associated with a teenager's sexual behavior

■ how to prevent, and cope with, sexual abuse: in the event that the teenager is the would-be or actual victim, and in the event that the teenager is the would-be or actual abuser

■ how to help a gay teenage child

■ at PCGC: treating teenage sex offenders

2. POPULARITY *(page 31)*

■ why popularity—or the lack of it—is such an important issue for teenagers

■ how to prevent, manage, and overcome problems associated with popularity or the lack thereof

■ guidelines for responding to a teenager's desire for cosmetic surgery

3. SCHOOL *(page 40)*

■ how to guide a teenager through the challenges and adult responsibilities of high school

■ how to determine if a teenager is having trouble studying and maintaining grades

■ when to allow extracurricular activities: the pros and cons

4. DEPRESSION *(page 48)*

■ causes and effects of depression in teenage children

■ how to prevent, manage, and overcome problems associated with teenage depression

■ how to detect and prevent a teenager's intention to commit suicide and what to do in the aftermath of a suicide attempt

■ at PCGC: the onset of adulthood

■ at PCGC: seasonal affective disorder

5. DISCIPLINE *(page 63)*

■ common disciplinary challenges presented by teenagers; emotional issues associated with those challenges

■ how to handle major teenage disciplinary problems

6. DIVORCE *(page 71)*

■ common teenage reactions to divorce

■ when one parent begins dating

■ how to prevent problems and encourage new relationships when one parent remarries

7. SUBSTANCE ABUSE *(page 80)*

■ common causes and effects of teenage abuse of controlled substances, including specific attention to the four most abused varieties: (1) alcohol, (2) amphetamines and barbiturates, (3) marijuana, and (4) cocaine

■ possible dangers associated with the use of specific drugs

■ how to detect whether a teenager is abusing drugs

■ how to help a teenager avoid, manage, and overcome substance-abuse problems

■ specific resources to contact for help in dealing with teenage substance abuse

8. RUNNING AWAY *(page 90)*

■ why teenagers run away

■ how to detect whether a teenager is planning to run away

■ how to discourage or prevent a teenager from running away

■ how to cope with running away when—and after—it happens

9. OVEREATING *(page 97)*

■ common causes and effects of teenage obesity and overeating

■ how to prevent, manage, and overcome teenage overeating problems

■ at PCGC: helping obese teenagers

10. PLANNING FOR THE FUTURE *(page 105)*

■ why it's important to develop plans for the future: college, vocational school, or work

■ how to prevent, manage, and overcome obstacles when a child "returns to the nest"

■ volunteer, work-study, and vocational programs that encourage exploration and choices for the future

■ establishing new relationships and limits as a teenager becomes an adult

11. PSYCHOTHERAPY *(page 113)*

■ how to determine if a teenager might need psychotherapy

■ how to choose an appropriate therapy and an appropriate doctor/ therapist

■ the meaning behind special diagnoses: depression, anorexia nervosa, and bulimia

Psychosomatic Illness

By definition, a psychosomatic illness is a genuine physical illness that has psychological as well as biological causes (*psycho*: the Greek root for mind; *soma*: the Greek root for body). More technically, such an illness is known as a *psychophysiological disorder*. As a rule, when the underlying psychological problem is effectively addressed, the physical symptoms of the illness are greatly alleviated and may even disappear.

The body and the mind are so interconnected that almost any illness can be said to have a psychosomatic component. However, certain stress-sensitive illnesses are commonly thought to be especially psychosomatic in nature, such as ulcers, headaches, stomachaches, asthma, high blood pressure, allergies, and skin rashes or blemishes (including acne).

Adolescence is a period of emotional and physical growth characterized by all sorts of new stress factors that have direct physical correlations. Among these factors are major and frequently unpredictable changes in body image; the onset of powerful new sexual feelings; and the demand for new or enhanced physical competencies (e.g., work skills, driving skills, athletic skills, and life-management skills).

Given all these new stress factors and their direct physical correlations, an adolescent is very likely to manifest new psychosomatic illnesses. She or he might also, or alternatively, experience the resurgence of former psychosomatic illnesses— even those that have not appeared since early childhood (something that often happens with asthma).

It's important for the parent of an adolescent who is troubled by such an illness to realize that the illness is real, not imaginary. However much you or your child may be creating stress that is contributing to the illness, neither of you is to blame for the illness itself. Instead, it is a natural process, and there are various ways that it can be successfully treated.

One of the most effective ways to manage or even cure many forms of psychosomatic illnesses involves biofeedback training. The sufferer is taught to recognize the link between emotions and physical symptoms, sometimes with the aid of computerized technology. Then behavior modification is employed to give the sufferer an increasing amount of control over the link. This behavior modification addresses both the emotions themselves and the physical reactions they help to produce.

Whenever you suspect that emotional factors may be contributing to your teenage child's illness, it's wise for you and your child to consult not only with a medical doctor but also with a psychologist or psychiatrist. This qualified professional can help both of you to "unlearn" patterns of transferring emotional stress to the body that might otherwise remain unconscious and unappreciated.

Autonomy Versus Intimacy

In referring to an adolescent child, psychologists and psychiatrists will often speak of the child's psychological capacity to be either *autonomous* (i.e., independent and self-reliant) or *intimate* (i.e., closely involved with another individual and dependent on her or him for emotional security). In general, this is known as the *autonomy versus intimacy* issue.

Depending on the situation at hand, the healthy adolescent is capable of achieving either autonomy or intimacy in an appropriate manner and with a minimum amount of difficulty. For example, a normal adolescent who spends increasing amounts of time with an agreeable companion will most likely develop an intimate friendship with that companion. Should the friendship dissolve either through irreconcilable differences or separation, the adolescent will be upset for a while but will will soon recover and enjoy life on her or his own until the time comes when a new friendship evolves. Similar patterns will develop with romantic partners, older mentors, or younger children that the adolescent takes care of.

By contrast, emotionally disturbed adolescents may suffer

severe difficulties being either autonomous or intimate, or they may assume autonomy or intimacy in a distinctly inappropriate way. For example, emotionally troubled adolescents may be unable to express their true feelings to their best friend. Indeed, they may not be able to form close friendships at all. Or they may become overly dependent emotionally on a mere acquaintance. When a relationship breaks up, they may be devastated and lonely for an alarmingly long period of time. Or they may toss off friendships and love affairs with a nonchalance that is bewildering to everyone around them.

If you suspect that your adolescent child has persistent difficulties forming intimate attachments or being independent— or problems in both areas—consider discussing the situation with a qualified professional. Such problems are better addressed early in your child's "adult" life than later.

At PCGC: Psychological Testing in Adolescence

Mental-health professionals, physicians, school personnel, and other specialists frequently make decisions that have a profound influence on teenage children. Historically, psychological testing has been a widely used and valued method for providing such professionals with the proper information to make those decisions.

Psychological testing is generally employed to determine individual differences and needs by providing specifics about a teenage child's abilities, strengths, personality style, and emotional functioning. It is also helpful in evaluating the actual or potential effects on teenagers of significant situational events, such as moving to a new home, coping with a serious illness, making the transition from junior high or middle school to high school, or going through a parental divorce.

For adolescents, psychological testing provides data about intellectual capacities, problem-solving strategies, neuropsychological processing, and personality organization. In addition, academic achievements are tested in order to assess the possible presence of learning disorders. Tests that PCGC frequently recommends or uses for personality evaluation include the Rorschach test (recently rejuvenated and rendered more useful by a research-based scoring system), the Thematic Apperception Test, Sentence Completion Tests, and (for adolescents age sixteen and older) the Minnesota Multiphasic Personality Inventory.

The experience of PCGC has shown that the more the family is informed about the testing and involved in the testing process, the more useful the evaluation is to them. Therefore, PCGC employs and advocates the following testing process:

■ The first step in the process is to help the child understand and appreciate the positive purpose of the testing: that is, to identify internal and external factors that may make living and learning easier for her or him.

■ Before the testing itself begins, the psychologist or test administrator meets with the child and parents to identify the reasons why testing is being sought, obtain relevant background history, address any initial questions or concerns the child and parents have, and explain the testing process.

■ It helps to have from two to four short, separate testing sessions rather than one long one. That way, fatigue factors are minimized, and a fuller range of the child's accomplishments and capabilities can be tested.

■ When testing is completed, the results are discussed with the family and the child.

For more information about psychological testing of adolescents, consult your physician, school counselor, or a local mental-health agency.

1.

Sexuality

The past twenty years have worked a revolutionary change in what it means to be a teenager, and by far the biggest impact has been in the area of sexuality. Thanks to medical and nutritional advances, teenagers today mature physically about two years earlier than their parents did, and the world within which this maturing process takes place harbors an unprecedented range of sex-related opportunities and dangers.

Sexual activity among teenagers today is less stigmatized and much easier to come by than it was for teenagers a mere generation ago. Therefore, it also begins at an earlier age and is more prevalent with each passing year. According to most expert polls and estimates, the majority of teenagers—males and females—are having regular sex (at least two or three times a month) by the time they are in eleventh grade.

At the same time, the potential risks involved in teenage sexual activity have escalated dramatically. One of the fastest-rising risk groups for acquired immune deficiency syndrome (AIDS) is teenagers. To date, no one has been known to recover after being infected with the HIV virus that leads to AIDS, and the average postinfection life span is four years.

Since 1989, according to the federal Centers for Disease Control in Atlanta, the number of reported cases of HIV infection among American teenagers has been doubling every fourteen months, with a much higher rate of heterosexual transmission than among adults. And while the current volume of teenage cases accounts for only 1 percent of the national total, about 20 percent of the latter are people in their early twenties. Many, if not most, of these people with AIDS in their early twenties are very likely to have contracted the infection—and, even more horrifying, to have spread it—unknowingly during their teenage years.

Besides the risk of AIDS during the teenage years, there's also the risk of other sexually transmitted diseases (STDs). The teenage rate for gonorrhea and syphilis, the most familiar STDs of the past, hasn't changed much in a generation. This is mainly because the ever-increasing numbers of gonorrhea and syphilis cases over the past twenty years have been detected and cured very early in their development, thus putting a limit on the spread.

However, the teenage rate of chlamydia, a little-known virus twenty years ago, has skyrocketed to become the most common STD in this age group. Currently it affects an estimated 25 percent of female teens and 15 percent of male teens.

Chlamydia is much more difficult to detect than gonorrhea and syphilis because it is more often asymptomatic—that is, the victim has no basis for suspecting that she or he is infected. Only about 20 percent of female teenagers infected with chlamydia actually suffer such physical indicators as abdominal pain, nausea, and/or a low fever. And an even smaller percentage of males afflicted with chlamydia actually suffer such physical indicators as painful urination or a runny discharge from the penis. Yet even in cases of chlamydia in which no symptoms present themselves, the long-range result can be sterility and/or widespread damage to the reproductive system and abdominal cavity.

Finally, there is the age-old problem of unwanted or inappropriate teenage pregnancy, which occurs more frequently today than it ever has in American history. The wider distribution and use of birth-control measures in recent years has simply failed to keep pace with the amount—and impulsiveness—of teenage sexual activity. Right now, one out of ten girls between the ages of fifteen and nineteen becomes pregnant, and half of the pregnancies result in childbirth. Each of these statistics represents a twofold jump over twenty years ago, and the situation shows every sign of getting worse with each passing year.

Emotionally speaking, the current, unprecedented increase in adolescent sexual opportunities and problems can subject the typical teenager to a much wilder roller-coaster ride than her or his parents experienced when they were teenagers. Because sexual activity is more commonplace among today's teenagers, so is the pressure to have sex and, if one becomes sexually active, to be a good sexual performer and to craft a personally satisfying sex life. Because the risk of contracting AIDS or chlamydia is much higher, so is the potential for fear, hysteria, and hostility. And because the odds of becoming a reluctant teenage mother or father are steadily increasing, so is the potential for life-crippling feelings of anger, guilt, and hopelessness.

To make the sex-related roller-coaster ride emotionally smoother for your teenager, try following these important guidelines:

■ *Educate yourself about sex-related issues that may affect your teenager*.

Always bear in mind that the situation you yourself faced as a teenager is *not* the same one that a teenage child today faces. Among the issues to become—and remain—informed about are the following:

■ sexual and romantic mores and customs among contemporary teenagers in general as well as among teenagers in your specific community;

■ sex-education programs that your child encounters or are available to your child at school, at religious organizations, or within the community;

■ birth-control options and resources;

■ options and resources available to teenage mothers- and fathers-to-be;

■ information regarding the transmission, prevention, and treatment of STDs, especially AIDS and chlamydia.

■ *Share with your child your own values regarding sex in general and your anxieties and preferences regarding her or his sexual life in particular.*

Be very honest and let your child know about your personal beliefs relating to romance and sex, your concerns relating to her or his romantic and/or sexual life, and how you would prefer that she or he behave. Don't keep your child guessing about where you stand and don't assume a guise of being more liberal—or more conservative—than you really are. In parent-to-child communication about sex, insincerity and a lack of candor can have disastrous consequences.

At the same time that you let your child know your feelings regarding her or his sex life, be careful not to translate these feelings into demands. Issuing ultimatums to your child regarding permissible attitudes and beliefs—whether they pertain to sex or to anything else—is inappropriate and potentially very harmful. It denies your child's rights to privacy and self-determination, leaves no room to disagree with you, and encourages secrecy and deception about what is really happening in case such knowledge might alienate you.

■ *Make sure that your child is informed about how to avoid common problems associated with sexual pressure or sexual activity.*

One of the biggest mistakes parents make with their teenage children is to advise them *what* problems to avoid without going one step further to advise *how* to avoid them. Through casual conversations, personal demonstrations, or even role-playing, try to encourage or even help your teenage child devise ways to do the following:

■ turn down unwanted sexual advances in a manner that best suits her or his personality and the situation at hand;

■ display a romantic interest in someone else in a respectful, nonintimidating manner;

■ recognize and respect someone else's rejection of her or his advances;

■ convey romantic feelings and expectations to her or his partner openly and honestly instead of letting them fester inside and misleading the partner;

■ elicit the romantic feelings and expectations of her or his partner in direct conversation instead of guessing them and being misled;

■ negotiate dating activities that are mutually agreeable as well as reasonably safe and responsible (e.g., that don't involve a high risk of being stranded somewhere or of winding up in unwanted company);

■ establish terms of intimacy with her or his partner that are physically safe, responsible, and respectful of both parties (if not abstention from sex, then the practice of safer sex).

■ *Encourage your child to be open with you about her or his feelings, attitudes, romantic interests, and relationships.*
Ask open-ended questions about your child's social life, that is, questions that invite casual, general discussion rather than a specific answer or a simple yes or no. For example, "What kind of relationship would you like to have with a boy?" or "Tell me about Mary—how are things going?" Listen calmly and nonjudgmentally to whatever your child tells you.

Above all, don't trivialize your child's romantic feelings no matter how humorous or absurd they may seem to you. For example, children in their early teens often develop strong crushes, usually on someone who is decidedly unattainable, such as a media star, a married teacher, or the much older sibling of a friend. Later, they may form seemingly obsessive attachments to individuals they barely know. However superficial or fantastical such feelings may appear to you, they are very real and important to your child. Indeed, they help her or him to experiment in a relatively safe context with a wide range of emotions and behaviors associated with love and sex.

An excellent way to maintain good communication with your child about romance, dating, and sex is to volunteer your own related experiences as a teenager whenever and however it is appropriate to do so. Offering such stories in a purely conversational manner can help your child better manage her or his own romantic or sexual life as well as bring you and your child closer together.

■ *Negotiate reasonable and clear policies with your child regarding her or his dating practices.*

Although it may not be advisable—or even possible—to force your beliefs about sex onto your child, it's very important to come to an agreement about practical matters associated with dating. Together with your child, set fair and workable policies regarding the following:

> ■ how and when you are to be informed about dates;

> ■ how and when you are to meet the people your child dates;

> ■ how many nights a week—and what nights—it is appropriate for your child to date;

> ■ how late at night your child can stay out on a date;

> ■ which dating spots and situations you consider to be "off limits";

> ■ what steps your child should be prepared to take during a date if an emergency or an undesirable situation arises (e.g., demanding to be taken home, calling home, calling a trusted friend or relative, getting a cab ride home, calling the police).

■ *Avoid always being negative when you talk about sex-related matters.*

Keep track of the times that you talk about sex-related matters with your child and make sure that these discussions don't repeatedly involve disparagements, warnings, fears, or prohibitions. A significant proportion of sex-related discussions with your child should be positive or at the very least neutral.

If, instead, your discussions are consistently negative, you may be sending a message to your child that you will categorically reject any positive or alternative sex-related feelings or information that she or he has to communicate. This kind of message is sure to inhibit your child from talking about sex at all and ultimately from valuing anything you have to say about sex.

■ *Whenever you and your child are talking about sex, be sure attention is paid to its emotional as well as its physical aspects.*

Your child needs to learn that any sexual involvement with another person has emotional repercussions for both partners. Help your child realize and appreciate this dimension of sexuality by referring to it every time you discuss sex.

Give your child a sense not only of the different emotions—pleasant and unpleasant—that she or he might experience in the course of various relationship scenarios but also of the feelings that her or his partner might experience. Impress upon your child that along with sexual desire comes the responsibility to manage that desire in a mature and thoughtful way and to ensure that the emotional well-being of both participants is respected and protected.

Puberty: The Great Divide

The factor that almost single-handedly marks the dividing line between childhood and adolescence is puberty. Regardless of a child's specific age, grade in school, personal responsibilities, or degree of social maturity, she or he cannot be considered an adult (or, more precisely, a person becoming an adult) until puberty has begun working its hormonal revolution in all aspects of the child's life. Parents of teenage children need to be particularly sensitive to their child's needs during this major transitional period in her or his development, for the very beginning of adulthood often determines how the eventual adult will turn out—not just physically, but also emotionally.

For girls, the onset of puberty is heralded by the first menstruation, which can occur anytime between the ages of nine and fifteen, although it usually takes place between the ages of nine and fifteen, although it usually takes place between the ages of eleven and thirteen. For boys, the beginning of puberty is more difficult to pinpoint. Like a female's ability to become fertile, a male's ability to fertilize (based on the potency of the sperm) can develop anytime between the ages of nine and fifteen, but it usually starts between the ages of thirteen and fifteen, slightly later than the typical beginning of menstruation for girls. Thus, boys are somewhat slower to mature physically than girls are.

To add to the puberty-period male's conscious or subconscious feelings of inferiority compared to the puberty-period female, the male is typically much slower than the female to manifest observable physical signs that he is, in fact, becoming

an adult. Secondary sexual characteristics brought on by puberty for a female include breast development, significant re-
distribution of body fat, and the growth of body hair. For a
male, they include the development of a slightly bulkier mus-
culature, the lowering of the voice's pitch, and the growth of
body hair. Overall, the average teenage male's comparative
uncertainty, insecurity, and sense of inferiority regarding the
timing and manifest signs of puberty could help prompt the
male-associated trend toward "lying" about sex-related status,
i.e., claiming more prowess or experience than one actually
has.

For both genders, the *emotional stress* triggered by the new
social issues accompanying puberty is just as significant as the
physical stress caused by the hormonal changes. With all the
changes they're experiencing in their bodies, children going
through puberty can become intensely concerned about peer
reaction. And because their self-esteem is so dependent on how
their peers regard them, this worry can't help but affect how
they feel about themselves personally. If a child is later than
usual to go through puberty, the concern and worry last longer
and take ever more desperate forms. This is particularly true
if the child's close friends start going through puberty at a
much earlier time or exhibit much more marked signs of physical development.

The following guidelines will help you help your child to
adjust to puberty more comfortably, whenever and however it
occurs:

■ *Avoid teasing your child about puberty.*
Tempting as it may be to help your child through an awkward
stage of life by trying to use humor, always remember that
your child is acutely sensitive during puberty about the image
she or he is projecting to other people. She or he can easily,
inexplicably, and unpredictably misinterpret even the most
well-meaning jests about her or his newly emerging identity.
And you may never realize that this is happening. A teenager
can be very skillful at concealing any hurt that others may
have caused.

■ *Treat puberty as a cause for joy.*
Take pride in the fact that your child has reached puberty,
and let her or him know that you feel proud. When talking
about puberty with your child, present it as a desirable and
positive stage of growth—linked with beauty, power, and a

rich new range of feelings. In your general conversations and remarks about adulthood, try to welcome your child into this new world, rather than making her or him feel awkward, fearful, ashamed, or regretful about leaving childhood behind. You might also consider arranging some sort of special occasion to honor your child's entry into adulthood: for example, an "adultlike" trip with both parents or the same-sex parent (no younger siblings!); a dinner at a fancy restaurant during which you bestow a special gift; or a formal "rite of passage" ceremony offered by your church, synagogue, or spirituality center.

■ *Don't assume that puberty automatically means that your child is more mature mentally, emotionally, or socially.*

For a time, your puberty-period child will have enough problems simply coming to terms with the physical aspects of puberty. Don't expect her or him to take on more adult perspectives, behaviors, and responsibilities right away. Society at large doesn't even treat an individual as an adult until she or he is twenty-one years old—at which time some physical changes associated with puberty are still taking place in most individuals. Instead, allow your child to mature mentally, emotionally, and socially at approximately the same rate as she or he did prior to puberty.

■ *Help your child to develop self-esteem, self-confidence, and social poise.*

Without being pushy, make an extra effort to encourage your child to engage in *solitary* activities that she or he performs well and that give her or him gratification. Doing so will assist your child to maintain an ongoing sense of competency, value, pleasure, and self-control as her or his physical and social image changes.

At the same time, and also without being pushy, help your child to seek information, instruction, and experiences that will enhance *social* skills. For example, you might try interesting her or him in reading young-adult-oriented books (indicated "YA" in libraries, bookstores, and book catalogues) or in subscribing to teen-related periodicals. Or you might suggest that your child take athletic lessons, attend summer camp, or participate in an all-adolescent environmental action project or hobby club.

Sexual Abuse in the Teenage Years

In the popular imagination, "child sexual abuse" is taken to refer to the molestation of prepubescent children. It's commonly thought that postpubescent children are physically, intellectually, socially, and emotionally so much more mature that they are far less likely to get into abusive situations, or if they do, to suffer from them.

In fact, the dramatic physical changes brought on by puberty are *not* accompanied by equally dramatic intellectual, social, or emotional changes. The latter changes take place at a much slower pace. Meanwhile, the postpubescent child, still insecure, unsophisticated, and dependent on others, remains vulnerable to the same types of abusive incidents and behavior patterns that are inflicted on prepubescent children.

According to the American Academy of Child and Adolescent Psychiatry, one out of every four females and one out of every ten males suffers sexual abuse before reaching the age of eighteen. And roughly half of the abuse victims at any given time are teenagers.

It's true that most cases of a teenage child being abused involve a long history of abuse by the same individual, often a family member, beginning well before the child entered puberty. But whether a child first encounters abuse *before* or *after* puberty, its emotional effects are the same in kind, and they can be similarly devastating in intensity. Aside from a confusing mixture of shame, guilt, fear, mistrust, anger, and hate, the victim is likely to develop a general and abiding sense of personal worthlessness. In a teenager, this feeling can easily lead either to sexual promiscuity or sexual frigidity.

Tragically, postpubescent children sometimes become perpetrators of sexual abuse of younger children. Most often the victim is a brother, sister, cousin, or child of a neighbor or friend: someone whom they encounter—and abuse—on a regular basis. Many of these teenage abusers were abused themselves as younger children, which helps to explain their behavior. Others were never abused but are tormented by various types of psychological problems, such as emotional abuse or deprivation at home or an overwhelming sense of personal failure and humiliation at school.

Listed below are separate sets of guidelines to follow relating to sex-abuse situations: "ABUSED" if you have reason to suspect that your teenage child is a victim of sexual abuse, and "ABUSER" if you have reason to suspect that your teenage child has sexually abused another child.

ABUSED

■ *Pay attention to signs that your child may have suffered sexual abuse.*
Among these signs are the following:

■ inexplicable bruises, scratches, or physical injuries;

■ depression or withdrawal from family or friends;

■ atypical aggressiveness and rage;

■ unusual avoidance of a particular individual or social situation;

■ dramatic change in attitude toward, or interest in, sex-related matters;

■ secretiveness;

■ uncharacteristic risk taking or suicidal behavior.

■ *Encourage your child to converse freely with you about any problem relating to sex abuse that she or he may be having.*
As much as possible, remain calm and allow your child a full opportunity to discuss not only her or his experiences but also how she or he *feels* about them. Don't interrupt with your own reactions or judgments until your child has fully spoken.
Always take any indication of sexual abuse very seriously. Assure your child that you believe her or him and that you understand her or his feelings about the situation.

■ *Reassure your child of her or his value as a human being.*
Children who have been sexually abused suffer from severely damaged self-esteem. Let your abused child know that you love her or him very much and that you are very proud of her or him for having the courage to talk to you about the abuse. Tell your child that whatever she or he has gone through is not her or his fault but the fault of the abuser.

Also, reassure your child about her or his future safety. Promise that you will do everything you can to make sure that the abuse doesn't happen again.

■ Contact the proper authorities immediately.

Before acting on your own to confront the abuser, get in touch with the proper authorities. They can help you plan the most effective strategy for making sure that the abuser never bothers your child—or another child—again; and they can offer such advice without requiring you to press charges or to face prosecution.

If the suspected abuse has occurred *within* the family, contact your local Child Protection Agency. If the suspected abuse has occurred *outside* the family, contact your local police department or district attorney's office.

■ Arrange for your child to be examined physically and emotionally.

Even an apparently mild form of sexual abuse can have serious physical and emotional consequences. As soon as possible, arrange for your child to see a physician for a medical checkup and a psychologist, psychiatrist, or qualified mental-health professional for an emotional evaluation.

ABUSER

■ Be alert for signs that your child may be sexually abusing another child.

Among these signs are the following:

■ unusual or problematic association with a younger child (e.g., your child spending a lot more time with a younger child than is customary, or consistently making the younger child cry);

■ seductiveness toward younger children;

■ secretiveness, especially in concert with a younger child;

■ estrangement from, and/or hostility toward, peers and adults;

■ excessive prurience or preoccupation with sexual matters;

■ possession of large amounts of pornography, especially depicting or describing forced sex and/or sex with younger children;

■ general aggressiveness toward others, with episodes of particular aggressiveness toward younger children;

■ marked increase in lying, stealing, or other forms of prohibited conduct.

■ *Ask your child about suspicious situations in a manner that encourages honesty and disclosure.*

Confront your child honestly and seriously with any reasons you have to believe that she or he may be abusing another child. Then help your child be straightforward with you by being a good, patient, and (for the time being) nonjudgmental listener.

Don't play games with your child by withholding information to see if she or he will corroborate it. This type of strategy only invites mistrust and resentment. Instead, be honest, direct, and concerned without being hostile.

When your child has finished telling you what she or he has to say and it's time for you to express your feelings about the matter, try not to lose your composure. Remember to direct all censure toward the bad *act* your child has committed, not toward your *child* her- or himself.

■ *Set rules and adopt measures aimed at preventing your child from getting into a potentially abusive situation.*

As much as possible, keep your child away from children she or he may be inclined to victimize or from situations that may invite seduction or abuse. Instead of leaving your child alone for extended periods of time, arrange for her or him to be supervised.

If you've established that there is someone in particular that your child has been sexually abusing, it is incumbent upon you to inform the parents of that child. Armed with such information, they can get medical and psychological care for their child and help you prevent your child from committing further acts of abuse.

Before you talk with the parents, it may be helpful to consult a qualified authority in child sexual abuse about how best to handle this type of exceptionally sensitive communication, given the particular situation and personalities involved. A consultation of this type will also give you additional courage and support for performing such a personally painful task.

■ *Help your child learn better self-control and more acceptable interpersonal behavior.*

Through conversations, carefully supervised social events, and even role-playing of specific real-life situations, help your child develop more respect for the rights of others and more skill at expressing her or his feelings in a respectable manner.

Assist your child in identifying and practicing better ways of achieving personal satisfaction in her or his relationships with others, such as working with others on a project, playing team sports, going with others to entertainment events, or competing against others for a particular honor. Encourage your child to use her or his *positive* interests and personality traits to form more lasting and mutually beneficial friendships with peers.

■ *Seek professional help for your child.*

Without question, a child who abuses another child sexually is suffering deep-rooted emotional problems. Her or his parents can use all the help they can get to address those problems as well as to come to terms with their personal feelings of outrage, guilt, shame, and disappointment.

If you are convinced that your child has been—or could be— sexually abusing children, don't hesitate to confer with a psychiatrist, psychologist, or other qualified mental-health professional. This person can evaluate your child's emotional health, work with her or him on specific psychological problems, and help you cope with your own pain and parental responsibilities under the circumstances.

Helping Your Gay Teenager

Being gay is typically not something that a teenager can accept without a certain amount of inner turmoil. There may be serious, if misguided, doubts: for example, "Am I gay because I love my best friend?" There may be denial: for example, "I'm just going through a strange phase right now." In fact, however, the prevailing estimate is that one out of every ten teenagers is genuinely homosexual, with an equal rate of incidence for males and females.

Homosexuality in itself is not a psychological illness, nor is it a matter of choice, except, perhaps, in the case of isolated acts of sexual experimentation. Rather, it is an affectional and erotic orientation toward the same sex, one that is as funda-

mental to a homosexual's psyche as an erotic orientation
toward the opposite sex is to a heterosexual's psyche.

Unfortunately, society at large, being 90 percent heterosexual, subjects homosexuals to a considerable amount of discrimination and persecution. It can be very difficult for parents of
a gay teenager to accept the fact that their child is so different
from them and so vulnerable to the prejudices of others. But
refuting, bemoaning, or rejecting their child's homosexual feelings will only add to their child's adjustment problems.

If your child appears to be gay or reveals her or his homosexual feelings to you, here are some guidelines for dealing
with the situation rationally, sensitively, and constructively:

■ *If you have good reason to believe that your child is gay
or is concerned about the possibility of being gay, don't
be afraid to initiate conversation on the topic.*

It's better to bring the issue out into the open than to let it
fester. Make your initial inquiries very tactful, general, and
open-ended. Ideally, use questions that can't be—and don't
have to be—answered with a simple yes or no.

Depending on the circumstances, a very impersonal approach
might be better: for example, "Many people develop strong,
sexual attractions toward members of their own sex. How do
you feel about this?" Or you may decide that the circumstances
warrant a more personal approach: for example, "There's something I want us to talk about so that we can be closer to each
other. Do you ever have sexual feelings toward (boys/girls)?"

Try to avoid using phrases like "Are you gay?" Instead, ask,
"Do you have sexual feelings toward (boys/girls)?" Adolescents
in particular—and people in general—occasionally have such
feelings without being predominantly gay. Either way, it's
important not to label your child "gay," or for that matter,
"straight." Let your child come to understand, and declare, her
or his own sexual identity.

In fact, throughout this initial conversation, try hard to be
a listener rather than a talker. And don't push things if your
child isn't forthcoming. At least you've opened up the subject
for discussion; you—or your child—can pick it up again later.

■ *Don't attack your child or your child's feelings.*

Given the way society stigmatizes homosexuality, teenagers
who suspect or know that they are homosexual are automatically susceptible to self-loathing, self-denial, depression, and
suicidal impulses. However unresolved your private feelings

may be, avoid inflicting even more emotional burdens on your child than she or he may already be carrying.

■ *Keep the lines of communication open.*

Most gay teenagers don't feel comfortable discussing their homosexuality with anyone, much less with a parent—at least until they themselves have sorted out their initial confusion about it. The resulting social isolation that gay teenagers suffer can be detrimental to this sorting-out process as well as devastating to their overall emotional well-being.

The more patient, nonjudgmental, and supportive you can be regarding your child and her or his highly sensitive sexual feelings and the more willing you are to listen whenever your child needs to talk about those feelings, the better it is for her or his psychological health. Avoid saying anything that makes your child feel rejected, makes you appear repulsed, or inhibits or precludes future discussions.

■ *Reassure your child of your love and of her or his value as a human being.*

Gay teenagers shouldn't be made to feel that their entire identity as individuals is defined by their sexual orientation. Nor should their parents withhold from them any demonstrations of love and regard until such a time as they "give up" being homosexual or resolve any confusion they may have about their sexuality one way or the other.

Such misguided strategies can only do harm, convincing gay teenagers that they are sexual freaks who may never be able to lead a worthwhile life. Instead, convince your child that she or he is loved and valued, and fully capable of having a fulfilling life, regardless of her or his sexual orientation.

■ *Avoid blaming yourself, someone else, or some situation for your child's homosexuality.*

No one knows what "causes" homosexuality. Quite likely it is just as rooted in biology and interpersonal chemistry as is heterosexuality.

Certainly no expert has ever been able to prove that an individual's homosexuality was the result of her or his mother or father being overly domineering, overly affectionate, overly distant, or otherwise at fault. Nor has it ever been established that casual experimentation with homosexuality transformed an otherwise straight individual into a gay one.

Furthermore, homosexuality is not, in itself, "blameworthy" except from a prejudicial point of view. Rather than worrying about what has caused—or is causing—your child to be or feel homosexual, accept the fact that your child is who she or he is, and feels what she or he feels, independent of who you are and how you feel.

Bear in mind that your role as a parent is to help your child become more self-aware and responsible so that she or he can lead a personally satisfying and productive life. You can't assume responsibility for your child's sexual orientation, but you can help your child come to terms with that orientation.

■ *Seek the support of sympathetic groups for your child and yourself.*

Contact local gay and lesbian organizations and encourage your child to do the same. Many areas have groups specifically designed to assist parents of homosexuals. (One major national group with many local chapters is called Parents and Friends of Lesbians and Gays [PFLAG].)

Whatever attitudes and emotions you and your child have toward homosexuality, both of you should be as well-informed about it as possible. And given the threat of social ostracism and gay bashing, you and your child should also have as substantial a network of potential supporters as possible.

CASE:

The Mother-Daughter Transfer

Four years after her divorce, Michele was going through another period of domestic warfare, this time with her thirteen-year-old daughter, Jody. The catalyst for the warfare was boys: Jody wanted to start dating them, they wanted to start dating Jody, and Michele was standing in their way.

"You're not old enough to date," Michele pronounced, and that was that as far as she was concerned. Jody, however, had some very powerful arguments on her side. Most of her close friends had already begun dating with their parents' permission, and these were parents whose opinions Michele had often admired and invoked in conversations with Jody.

In all other child-raising matters involving rules and rights, Michele had been remarkably successful. From time to time Jody would initially rebel against a particular policy, but in every case she soon acknowledged the wisdom of that policy and cooperated with it.

This time was dramatically different. For the past two months Jody had been actively fighting Michele to lift her ban on dating; instead of diminishing in intensity, the fights were getting steadily worse and worse. After an especially ugly shouting match, they agreed to seek help from a family therapist.

Michele discovered that she was going through a common experience for a parent of a just-datable teenager, namely, being haunted by ghosts from the past: the ghost of one's own just-datable teenage self and the ghosts of one's own parents at that time. The more Michele examined her nay-saying behavior with Jody, the more she realized that she had been automatically reenacting her own and her parents' fears about males and about love when she herself first began dating. Subconsciously, these fears now seemed even more justified to her in hindsight, given the trauma of her recent divorce.

The therapist explained to Michele that almost all parents occasionally project their own childhood experiences, perceptions, and sensibilities onto their children and occasionally lapse, against their will, into the same parenting style that their parents modeled for them. However, the tendency to do so can be much stronger and much more unconscious when their children reach dating age. Suddenly, the parents are subject to all sorts of mixed emotions. These emotions include not only *fear* (regarding possible harm to, as well as possible loss of control over, their child) but also *jealousy* (aimed at anyone who might capture their child's affections), *envy* (aimed at their child, whose youthful adventures are just beginning), and *grief* (regarding the upcoming "loss" of their child's innocence).

Understanding these psychological dynamics in her relationship with Jody helped Michele be more realistic about the dating issue. She could see that the real question facing her was not *whether* Jody should date but *how* Jody should date. Thereafter, Michele was much less overbearing in her conversations with Jody about dating. And while it was some time before Jody actually began dating, the fights over it ceased almost immediately.

At PCGC:
Treating Teenage Sex
Offenders

Many teenage sex offenders were victims of sexual abuse themselves when they were younger. Indeed, psychiatrists and psychologists now consider that a personal history of sexual abuse
is one of the most common factors influencing a teenage child
to abuse other children in a similar way. Treating teenage
sexual offenders thus becomes a matter of interrupting a destructive, sex-related cyclical pattern in the offender's behavior.

But effective therapy for teenage sex offenders doesn't stop
there. It must also address other destructive cyclic patterns in
the offender's behavior so that the offender learns to manage
each interdependent aspect of her or his personal life more
maturely and successfully. This comprehensive approach to
therapy, administered relatively early in the offender's life,
greatly reduces the risk that she or he will continue to create—
or suffer—serious sex-related problems of any type during the
rest of adolescence and adulthood.

Finally, effective therapy for teenage sex offenders needs to
address the manner in which the teenager's environment contributes or reacts to the offensive behavior. Besides involving
the teenager's parent(s) or parental substitute(s) and other
family members, effective therapy may have to extend to the
teenager's friends, teachers, school administrators, and personnel from other agencies that already have—or could have—
a significant impact on the teenager's life.

One example of this type of comprehensive approach to therapy is PCGC's Adolescent Sex Offender Treatment Program.
A five-person treatment team, including a child psychiatrist
and a clinical psychologist, works directly with each client to
develop appropriate strategies for eliminating the offending
behavior. It also works both directly and indirectly with the
offender's family and community to set up and support these
strategies.

Specific treatments administered by the program include
individual counseling, family therapy sessions, group meetings for the offenders, and group meetings for the parents, or

parent substitutes, of offenders. Other services available on
an as-needed basis are psychiatric consultation, medication
clinic, and psychological evaluation.

All treatments in the program focus on the client's sexuality
but deal with other relevant issues as well. For example, the
group meetings address socialization issues, such as peer relationships, school problems, and preparation for employment
and independence. Family therapy concentrates on supporting
parental competence in handling the child's inappropriate behaviors through the restructuring of family roles and relationships and the development of more effective family
management skills.

Families of teenage sex abusers often initiate their own
referral to the PCGC's Adolescent Sex Offender Program.
Other referrals come from the state's Department of Human
Services, mental-health centers, and individual professionals
in the mental-health field.

If your child, or a child you know, might benefit from this
type of program, ask your psychiatrist, psychologist, or mental-
health professional whether a similar program exists in your
area. If not, seek therapy that has the potential of involving
family members and community members.

2.
Popularity

It's not difficult for parents to appreciate a teenage child's interest in being popular among peers of the same sex. What's difficult for them to appreciate is that a teenage child can so often place a higher value on the opinions of friends than on the opinions of her or his parents—or, for that matter, of society as a whole. Just for the sake of being popular within a special group, a basically sensible teenager may willingly and enthusiastically engage in foolish, harmful, and even criminal behavior.

For the vast majority of children between the ages of thirteen and twenty, male or female, peer approval is enormously important. During the eighth and ninth grades in particular, it can be the single most valued factor in a child's life. The reason for this does not lie as much in the desire for friendships in themselves as it does in the desire to be an accepted member of a group.

Caught in an awkward transition period between childhood and adulthood, teenagers are psychologically insecure as individuals—much more so than during the so-called latency period that extends roughly from age six to age twelve. Membership in a specific group of peers brings with it a precious feeling of being worthy as a person, having social power, and belonging somewhere in the world outside the family.

In fact, being popular is such a major issue for teenagers in general that it's often a sign of emotional problems if an individual teenager is *not* a fiercely involved member of a particular group of peers. This doesn't mean that a teenager who is solitary by nature or circumstance can't still be emotionally healthy; but such an individual is definitely the exception rather than the rule.

Most teenagers who are not a part of a "pack" suffer a great deal of emotional distress, not from being unpopular per se but from experiencing specific incidents of subtle or blatant rejection. In many cases, a teenager's preexisting emotional problems, such as extreme shyness or aggressiveness, inspire rejection by her or his peers, and so the rejected teenager winds up becoming doubly troubled.

As far as experts have been able to determine, the desire to be popular is just as intense in teenage boys as it is in teenage girls. However, there are some minor, gender-related distinctions.

Western culture permits—and on certain occasions, such as social gatherings, even expects—females to be more expressive and demonstrative than males regarding their friendships. Thus, in comparison to their male counterparts, teenage girls tend to *appear* more enthusiastic and effusive during times when they are secure about their popularity and more depressed and antagonistic when they are insecure about it.

Moreover, peer bonding among teenagers usually manifests itself in different ways, according to whether the group is all male or all female. Teenage girls tend to reinforce their group identity by trying to *look like each other*. Teenage boys in a group might find themselves imitating each other in appearance, but such occasions are much less frequent and considerably less meaningful than they are for girls. After all, the total range of culturally acceptable appearance possibilities for males of any age is relatively narrow as opposed to the total range for females. In contrast to teenage girls, teenage boys tend to derive a stronger sense of group identity simply by *hanging around each other*.

One popularity-related characteristic that is common to both teenage boys and teenage girls is a strong preference for keeping the world of friends and that of home as separate as possible. This makes it extremely challenging for parents to get a good working sense of what is actually happening in their teenage child's social life outside the home. Even the most honest and family-oriented teenagers will occasionally resort to secrecy and misrepresentation when it comes to talking to their parents about their friends.

Teenagers have a right—and a need—to be granted a certain measure of privacy in conducting their peer relationships. It enables them to test their independent capacity to get along with others and to experiment with attitudes, behaviors, and pursuits that differ from the ones prevailing in the home environment. Thus, parents of a teenager have to accept the fact that some sort of information gap will always exist between them and their child regarding the latter's friends. Nevertheless, parents of a teenager are still responsible for doing whatever they reasonably can to keep their child from being harmed or from harming others.

In dealing with your teenage child's popularity-based concerns, you'll probably have little choice but to be exceptionally tactful and watchful. Assuming that your child is devoted to a particular group of friends, you must try as best you can to learn more about that group—its other members, its activities, and its norms—without offending your child or inspiring deception. Assuming your child clearly suffers from *not* being a popular member of a group, you must try to find out why your child isn't popular without causing her or him undue embarrassment. In either case, you must use the knowledge you gain with great care so that you can step in to help your child whenever it's appropriate, without inadvertently making matters worse.

Here are guidelines to assist you in these complicated endeavors:

■ *Set reasonable rules and policies regarding your child's social life.*

Your child should know the parameters within which she or he is free—and trusted—to operate. Meet with your child for the specific purpose of setting these parameters and do so again whenever circumstances warrant reinforcement or renegotiation.

Among the rules and policies to consider are the following:

■ Establish the times when you expect your child to be home (e.g., for meals, to do homework or chores, or to go to bed).

■ Establish how many evenings—and what evenings—during the week it's permissible for your child to socialize with friends.

■ Agree upon a standard procedure that each of you will follow to let the other one know what you are doing and—if possible— how you can be reached (e.g., by always leaving a note when you can't tell the other one orally or by making sure to telephone if you're away from home for a longer period of time than you anticipated).

■ Let your child know that you expect arrangements to be made for you to meet her or his friends at an early stage of the relationship (e.g., by inviting the friend home to dinner).

■ State clearly anything that your child is not allowed to do with peers (e.g., go to a place where alcohol is being served or leave the city limits without permission).

■ *Keep track of your child's day-to-day activities.*

Monitor where your child goes, with whom (if anyone), and what she or he does by questioning her or him directly. Note any patterns of behavior that emerge in your child's social life over time, such as a long period of being alone, socializing with the same person, or spending hours just roaming around the mall with friends. When you put these patterns together with other factors in your child's life, they may prove to be significant.

Try to avoid being dictatorial or judgmental in monitoring your child's purportedly "free" time but don't abandon your need to know.

Teenagers are so self-absorbed by nature and so inclined to forget—
or avoid—keeping their parents informed, that it's dangerously easy
to lose touch with what's happening in their lives.

■ *As often as practical, observe how your child plays and socializes.*

The more you watch how your child interacts with others when she
or he isn't especially conscious of being observed, the better idea you
will have of her or his overall emotional maturity and security in
social situations as well as particular social habits, inclinations, resources, talents, and problems.

Avoid outright spying on your child by, for example, eavesdropping
on conversations, reading her or his mail, or following her or him
clandestinely. If you do spy on your child, you risk making both of
you suspicious about each other and destroying any trust between
you. Should specific circumstances seem to warrant such intrusions
into your child's privacy, consider seeking advice from a mental-health
professional before taking any action you may regret.

■ *Take your child's concerns about popularity seriously.*

Whether or not you're able to agree with your child in matters having
to do with popularity, or lack thereof, always take a sympathetic
interest when she or he talks to you about such matters. More than
anything else, it's crucial for you to understand what's important to
your child and for your child to feel that you do understand.

Above all, guard against dismissing or ridiculing your child's friendships or lack of them. A teenager is especially susceptible to feeling
disregarded, embarrassed, or humiliated and may not respond well to
even the most innocuous and well intended teasing. Try to treat your
child—and any friends she or he may make—at least as seriously as
you expect her or him to treat you and your friends.

■ *Offer advice in a casual, nonjudgmental manner.*

Being a tactful, supportive, and good listener in conversations about
popularity with your child does *not* mean that you can't give her or
him advice. Teenagers often use such conversations to "think out
loud," and they actually want feedback from their parent.

For example, if your child expresses dissatisfaction with a certain
group of friends, she or he may be indirectly seeking a push from you
to leave that group. If you sincerely feel that such an action is warranted, then by all means let your child know—just as you would one
of your own, same-age confidants in a similar situation.

Don't insist that your child follow your advice or imply that she or
he would be foolish not to do so. But do go ahead and share your

experience and opinions whenever this course of action seems appropriate.

■ *Be alert for signs of possible trouble.*

If you observe any of the following negative patterns, bring it to your child's attention as a pretext for having a calm but serious discussion about the nature of her or his social life:

> ■ chronic violation of "house rules," especially with one particular friend or group of friends;

> ■ a dramatic change in your child's attitude, behavior, physical state, or emotional state that is adversely affecting her or his school life or family life (e.g., pronounced and frequent fatigue, impatience, use of foul language, distractedness, or rebelliousness);

> ■ repeated episodes of otherwise inexplicable anger, withdrawal, or depression;

> ■ repeated incidents when your child has suffered serious physical or emotional hurt, especially from one particular child or group;

> ■ repeated incidents when your child—or your child's group—has inflicted serious physical or emotional hurt upon another child, especially one particular child;

> ■ a dramatic and inexplicable change in your child's apparent financial status (i.e., unusual wealth, poverty, or need for substantial amounts of money);

> ■ frequent and escalating incidence of lying and/or stealing;

> ■ radical, adverse change in your child's ethical and moral standards as evidenced by her or his statements or conduct;

> ■ perseverance in not letting you meet her or his friends even after several direct requests from you.

■ *Consistently work to bolster your child's self-esteem and self-reliance.*

The more teenagers value themselves and their independence, the less susceptible they are to the pressures and problems associated with popularity or the lack thereof. Express your love and admiration to your child frequently. Guide her or him toward activities and interests that will nourish her or his pride, self-confidence, and appreciation of solitude.

■ *Consider seeking professional help for especially problematic situations.*

In order to be popular, or to cope with not being popular, a teenager can get into all sorts of serious trouble. Beyond simply failing in school, alienating the family, and becoming deeply depressed, there are the myriad dangers of substance abuse, compulsive sex, suicidal thrill seeking, or such crimes as stealing, assaulting, raping, destroying property, or disturbing the peace.

If your child seems caught in a pattern of negative behavior and nothing you do seems to help, don't hesitate to consult with a psychiatrist, psychologist, or qualified mental-health professional. This individual can offer both you and your child vital, even lifesaving support.

Interpersonal Versus Intrapersonal Intelligence

In psychological and psychiatric terms, "*inter*personal intelligence" refers to a child's knowledge and skills involving social relationships. By contrast, "*intra*personal" intelligence refers to a child's knowledge and skills involving her or his own, inner self—independent of the outside world.

A teenager with a high degree of interpersonal intelligence is one who makes friends easily, can lead others effectively, and can cooperate, compromise, and resolve conflicts within a group context. Interpersonal intelligence tends to be acquired by extensive socialization in a variety of contexts, such as assuming an active role in a large family, engaging in different types of play and competition with diverse friends, and performing tasks in concert with other individuals and work teams.

A teenager with a high degree of intrapersonal intelligence is one who is adept at cultivating self-knowledge as well as knowledge for the sake of personal development, is capable of enjoying solitude for extended periods of time, and can identify her or his personal needs, motivations, and feelings apart from those of others.

Every child has some degree of both types of intelligence, but most children become more intelligent in one of these two ways than in the other. Typically, a child who is extroverted by nature will wind up having a better-developed interpersonal intelligence; one who is introverted by nature will wind up having a better-developed intrapersonal intelligence.

As a result, extroverted children often suffer psychological problems because of a deficiency in intrapersonal intelligence (i.e., a lack of knowing their "inner selves"). Introverted children generally have the opposite problem: They suffer psychological problems because of a deficiency in interpersonal intelligence (i.e., a lack of knowing how to interact effectively with others).

When such imbalances are first detected by parents or educators, they are often treated inappropriately. Simply pressuring an apparent bookworm into joining a soccer team to become more interpersonally intelligent could easily backfire. The bookworm may experience so much unpleasantness and even trauma playing soccer that she or he will retreat even further into books. The same kind of thing might happen if a soccer lover is forced to read the complete works of Shakespeare in order to become more intrapersonally intelligent. The soccer lover's dislike of reading may instead be reinforced.

Much can be done to correct a troubled child's imbalance in interpersonal versus intrapersonal intelligence, but it must be done carefully, with full respect for the child's personal capabilities and vulnerabilities. Fortunately, most psychologists and psychiatrists are well qualified to assist individual children (along with their parents, teachers, and caretakers) in identifying the particular training methods and experiences that will most help them develop the type of intelligence they lack.

Cosmetic Surgery: Yes or No?

As cosmetic surgery becomes increasingly easier, quicker, more comfortable, and less expensive, more and more teenage girls and boys are seeking it to solve what they consider life-disfiguring problems with their appearance. Among the more common flaws that teenagers hope to correct are bumpy noses, receding chins, or large, floppy ears, but the list also includes everything from tiny moles to sunken cheekbones to large breasts.

For the dissatisfied teenager, the issue pretty much boils

down to this: "I would be so much more attractive and therefore popular if I only had [desired version of feature] instead of [feature in its present state]." Cosmetic surgery seems a simple and clear-cut matter. For the dissatisfied teenager's parent, however, the issue of whether to undertake surgery is far more problematic.

In the first place, the parent is almost always unable to see the offending feature in quite the same light as the teenager. To the typical parent in such a situation, the feature in question just doesn't appear significantly unattractive. In many cases, the parent actually possesses the identical feature, in which case its rejection by the teenager can be almost insulting.

In the second place, the parent knows from her or his greater experience in life that altering the way one looks—however dramatically—is not guaranteed to help one gain, retain, or increase one's personal popularity. Nor is it certain to provide the same sense of private, inner satisfaction that one might have anticipated.

In the event that your child expresses an interest in having cosmetic surgery, keep the following tips in mind:

■ *Acknowledge your child's concern.*

Although cosmetic surgery may strike you as an absurd or impractical course of action, your child takes it quite seriously. And behind that seriousness lurk complex emotions—including embarrassment, self-hatred, pride, and ambition—that deserve your sympathy and attention.

Listen thoughtfully and respectfully to what your child has to say about the matter. Indicate that you understand her or his frustration. Ask questions that will help both of you put the issue into a fuller, more realistic perspective: for example, "What has happened to make you feel that [the feature] is unattractive?" and "How long have you felt this way?"

■ *Reassure your child of your love and high regard.*

Tell your child that you care deeply for her or him regardless of how she or he looks. In addition, tell your child that the feature she or he personally finds so bothersome does not seem unattractive to you and may, in fact, not seem unattractive to others. In many cases, this type of reassurance, especially from several different sources, succeeds in putting off any further consideration of cosmetic surgery.

■ *Seek evidence to support or refute the argument for cosmetic surgery.*

First and foremost, talk with and observe your child to determine how deeply she or he is troubled by the offending feature. Is it causing serious and lasting emotional problems, or is it, instead, a source of *occasional* worry and frustration? Assuming the former is true, the case for surgery is stronger. Does the feature itself genuinely seem to be the focus of your child's displeasure, or is it instead merely a convenient symbol for some other, more complicated issue? Again, assuming the former is true, the case for surgery is stronger.

Next, discuss with your child what, specifically, she or he anticipates will happen *after* the surgery: How and why will life be different from the way it is now? If your child's expectations seem illogical or inflated, then the case for surgery is weaker.

Finally, give careful thought to how your child has behaved in the past regarding matters of personal appearance. Has your child repeatedly changed her or his mind about preferred hairstyles, clothing, and other forms of personal adornment? Has your child frequently gone through brief periods of dissatisfaction or disappointment with the way she or he looks, targeting different features at different times? If the answer to either of these questions is yes, then you have grounds for not wanting to go ahead with the surgery.

■ *Proceed slowly and cautiously.*

Assuming both you and your child come to agree that cosmetic surgery is a viable possibility, wait at least a couple of years, if possible, before having it done. You and your child both need to bear in mind that cosmetic surgery will create an irrevocable difference in your child's appearance. Therefore, it's reasonable to test your child's resolve to have cosmetic surgery by postponing any action for an extended period of time. If your child reiterates a desire for the surgery several times during this waiting period, then you can be more assured that she or he is committed to it and will accept the results.

In some situations, waiting may be a necessity. Very rarely is it advisable to undergo cosmetic surgery before the feature being altered has reached its full growth. Ears, for example, are usually fully developed by the time a child reaches adolescence; but the nose may continue to evolve until age fifteen; the chin, until age twenty.

3.

School

Moving from elementary school to middle school, junior high, or high school has a major impact on an adolescent's emotional life. It lands her or him in a quasi-adult, multidimensional world that is typically much more socially challenging, emotionally frustrating, and intellectually daunting than elementary school ever was.

Adolescents are more independent in general and more responsible for their scholastic and social success or failure in school than younger children, who still feel primarily attached to the family and home environment. Teenage students have more freedom to make decisions about classes, homework, and school-related activities. They also relate to classmates and teachers on a more complex and mature basis. Overall, each and every teenage student faces a new, expanded scope for creating and standing upon her or his own reputation, and rightly feels both threatened and exhilarated by the prospect.

During their school years, teenagers are in the process of preparing to leave home permanently to begin their lives as self-sufficient adults. Ideally, both home and school will work in harmony to foster the emotional growth needed to achieve this goal. When home life and school life are *not* in harmony, teenagers, by switching back and forth between what is expected of them in each separate environment, can suffer great emotional turmoil. Already caught in a stage of life where they are neither fully adults nor fully children, adolescents can be even more overwhelmed if they are treated as independent and reliable beings in one world and dependent and untrustworthy beings in the other.

During the first few months while teenagers are making the transition from elementary school to middle school or junior high, it is not unusual for academic performance to suffer and for emotional difficulties to emerge. In most cases, the adolescent student's new school life will have a more varied and demanding curriculum, an increased amount of homework, a greater number of teachers and classmates to get to know, and many more extracurricular activities from which to choose. The same sort of "shifting period" usually occurs between middle school or junior high and high school, although to a slightly lesser degree. But, after three or four months of transition, if a student's academic performance continues to be worse than normal, and if her or his emotional difficulties fail to ease up, there may be serious psychological problems in the making.

As the parent of an adolescent student, you need to be on the alert for this sort of situation. And even if it doesn't occur, you always need to know as much as you can about your child's school environment so that you can take effective steps to ensure that your teenager's home life and school life are in productive harmony with each other. Here are suggestions to help you in this effort:

■ *Know your school's curriculum and keep in close touch with your child's teachers and counselors.*

Attend as many of the parent-teacher meetings, conferences with academic advisers, and other parent-oriented activities as you can. If the school relies on parent volunteers for coaching extracurricular activities, chaperoning social functions, or serving on fund-raising programs, take advantage of these opportunities to get involved in your teenager's school. Teachers and counselors who know the parents of the students they work with often take more time and interest in those students' progress and are quicker to consult with parents when problems arise.

Meet with your child's guidance counselor early in the first year to talk over the requirements for graduation. Many schools have minimal graduation requirements that may not be sufficient or appropriate for college-bound students. You can help your teenage daughter or son adjust to school more easily if you have a good sense of the range of academic programs that are available and of which programs may be the most appropriate for her or his future plans.

Knowing firsthand as much as you can about the school will equip you all during the year to initiate conversations with your teenager about what's going on at school. It's essential to have other, more specific openers than the standard "How was school today?" to which most teenagers will usually give a begrudging, uninformative answer like "Fine," "Okay," or "The usual." Your teenager will feel compelled to share with you more relevant information if you have personal knowledge of, and involvement with, the faculty and programs.

■ *Learn as much as you can about your child's teachers and what she or he thinks of them.*

Your child's academic progress hinges to a great extent on the teachers and your child's relationships with them. Younger teenagers admire fairness in a teacher and a willingness to help with problems. Older teenagers also cite fairness as an important issue, but in addition they are concerned about a teacher's knowledge, instructional competence, and enthusiasm. Older students realize that their chances at college and future employment depend on their teachers' expertise and ability to motivate.

If your child is having trouble with a teacher, don't tell her or him to ignore the teacher and concentrate on the subject matter. The teacher's personality is intimately woven into the subject matter and the way it is presented in class. If your teenager claims that a teacher plays favorites, is abusive or insulting, appears to be uninterested in the subject (or in teaching itself), or anything else that suggests incompetence, don't hesitate to investigate. Meet with the teacher or school authorities to resolve the issue. The quality of your child's education hangs in the balance.

■ *Get involved as soon as possible if your teenager becomes a discipline problem at school.*

If your teenage child is misbehaving at school—disrupting or cutting classes, starting fights with other students, or engaging in vandalism—it is likely that she or he is also not doing well academically. The two often go hand in hand. Usually such misbehavior hides feelings of inadequacy or lack of acceptance. Ironically, even though other students will give the troublemakers the attention they seek—by talking about them or, in the case of the class clown, laughing about their exploits—the attention is thin and ultimately not satisfying. Most students will admit that they don't like the disruptive behavior and they don't feel comfortable being close friends with the troublemakers themselves.

Try to discover and understand the underlying problems when you first learn that your son or daughter is causing trouble in the classroom. More attention and acceptance at home can often ease the situation at school. It is extremely important that you as a parent address the situation, since teachers frequently don't have the time, patience, or sensitivity to help disruptive students individually. Many teachers simply resign themselves to the situation and wait out the semester until the troublemaking student moves on to another class.

■ *Help your teenagers with their homework without doing it yourself.*

Be supportive of your child's need for help with homework, but never do the homework yourself. Perfectly written homework assignments are misleading to the teacher if they reflect *your* level of knowledge and understanding, not your child's. Parents who do homework for their teenagers also encourage a dependency that the adolescent years are meant to gradually reduce.

Tutoring your children is an activity that goes beyond occasionally helping them with their homework, as needed, to assuming the role of their teacher on a regular and ongoing basis. You should be very careful about assuming this role. In the case of adolescent children in particular, it can create confusion in the parent-child relationship, which should be based on love and acceptance, not academic performance. Putting yourself in the position of criticizing your child and correcting mistakes on school subjects may easily generate tension that neither you nor your teenager need. Also, bear in mind that teaching methods, even subjects and content, change over the years. Your own grasp of a subject may be outdated, and your own method of presentation may be at cross purposes with the teacher's. If tutoring appears necessary, you can try doing it on your own for a while, to see if it works. However, it may be better in the long run to engage the help of a professional tutor. Your school guidance department should have specific suggestions.

■ *Encourage and motivate your teenagers to do well in school without putting undue pressure on them to excel beyond their natural capacities.*

Show interest, support, and encouragement for all of your teenager's school activities, without making your child think that she or he needs to be at the top of the class to win your approval. Putting too much pressure on teenagers to "be the best" can be self-defeating, while it takes the fun and enjoyment out of school. Most important of all, avoid bribing or threatening your child to do well, or even better, if "better" is clearly beyond your child's natural talents and intellectual capacities. Instead, motivate your child to want to do the best that she or he can. This is much more effective than getting your child to study out of fear or failure.

Children should never be working just to please their parents—or, for that matter, anyone else, including their teachers. Otherwise, they may end up never taking chances, pushing themselves to be more creative, or accepting new projects, out of a fear that they might do something "wrong."

Learn how to inquire about your adoelscent child's schoolwork and assignments without being too inquisitive or snoopy. At all costs, avoid nagging your child or giving the impression of nagging (try to see your discussions from your child's point of view), because many teenagers will refuse to talk at all about what's going on at school if they think such conversations are likely to result in nagging.

■ *Take a reasonable and consistent approach to grades.*

For all their significance, grades are not the most important thing in the world. Good grades do not assure success later in life, nor do poor grades guarantee future failure. And yet they tend to exert an all-controlling influence over the adolescent student's self-imposed educational efforts. In survey after survey, a majority of middle school, junior high, and high school students admit that they study primarily to get good grades, rather than to learn the material. In some surveys, over 50 percent of the students admit to cheating now and then, usually because it's the only way they think they can achieve a good grade.

Try not to give your child mixed messages about grades. You can easily confuse a child if you sometimes tell her or him to study hard and do well on tests because grades are important, while other times you say that grades are not all that important. Avoid extreme statements and overgeneralities in either direction.

Parents of teenagers also tend to give mixed messages about excelling in school at all costs, and, at the same time, living ethically by a strict code of honesty that forbids cheating and cutting corners. Many students cannot always square these two demands, especially if they see parents and other adults trying to "get ahead" by violating similar codes of honesty: for example, by cheating on their income taxes, by telling little white social lies, or by driving above the speed limit. The excuse that "everybody does it" encourages teenagers to break the rules, especially in the interests of a worthy goal like graduating from high school with good grades.

■ *Have your teenager checked for learning disabilities if she or he consistently does poorly in school.*

Usually learning disabilities are discovered in elementary school. However, it is not uncommon for children to reach adolescence without discovering that their so-so performance in school has, in fact, been partially due to an undetected learning disability. The most common ones of this type include hearing impairment, poor vision, and neurological problems (such as Attention Deficit Hyperactivity Disorder) that prevent concentration—all of which can get progressively more severe as the child ages. If these problems are not diagnosed early, children might be reading four or five years below their chronological age by the time they reach high school.

If your teenager persistently skips class or fails to do homework for no apparent reason, this may be a sign of an undetected learning disorder. Similarly, chronic underachievement, even in subjects that an adolescent seems to be interested in, can also indicate a learning disability, rather than "laziness" or "slow development," which is how underachievement is often explained. If your child shows consistently poor performance, arrange for testing to determine the cause. Your school guidance counselor can help.

■ *Make a special effort to create a supportive and encouraging home environment.*

Generally, teenagers who come from home environments that are intellectually stimulating, are conducive to study, and take advantage of educational opportunities in the community do better than students who do not come from such environments. Create a favorable home life by taking interest in your teenager's studies, talking about current events, and making use of community museums, art galleries, movies, nature centers, and political events.

Also share with your teenage child those aspects of your own life that relate to her or his school life, such as being reviewed by supervisors at work, preparing reports for business meetings, getting along with co-workers, worrying about failure, or handling success. Adolescents are in the process of moving into the adult world, and ideally their school experience is preparing them for that move. You can facilitate this transition by showing them parallels between their school activities and adult life situations.

The Pros and Cons of Extracurricular Activities

Many adults look back fondly on the extracurricular activities they engaged in as teenage students. Indeed, they often regard those experiences as the most memorable and satisfying ones of their school years. And frequently those experiences deserve that place of honor. Far from being something extra, as the word "extracurricular" implies, activities such as sports, music, drama, debate, photography, and school politics are considered by many educators and parents to be an integral part of the holistic learning that should take place during adolescence.

School clubs and organizations can provide teenagers with valuable skills, attitudes, and lessons in life that they cannot get in the standard classroom environment. It's a good idea to encourage your adolescent child to join at least one nonacademic activity to supplement and enrich her or his basic classroom education. There are, however, pros and cons in considering how many activities a child should engage in, and how extensively these activities should be permitted to shape the child's overall development.

PROS:

■ Extracurricular activities can develop school loyalty among students. The additional time that students spend at school for such activities and the expanded opportunities that they're given for meeting other students and teachers outside of a classroom setting combine to stimulate a deeper interest in, and commitment to, the school.

■ Nonclassroom programs foster constructive teamwork among students. Even when the activity is competitive in nature, or requires tryouts, such as sports, drama, chorus, or orchestra, students learn to appreciate a wider range of skills and talents than that required in the traditional academic competition of taking tests and getting grades, and they learn more ways of accepting their one-time competitors as models, collaborators, or even better friends.

■ Adolescents develop deep and rewarding relationships with the adults who serve as coaches, moderators, and advisers for the extracurricular programs. This can be valuable preparation for their future relationships with employers and co-workers. It also gives adolescents alternative counselors to seek out when they need help with academic or personal problems.

■ Students involved in extracurricular activities come to know a wide range of other students. School clubs and organizations provide a relaxed, informal atmosphere for meeting like-minded friends, which can be a help for a student who is not forthcoming in class because of poor academic skills or who is naturally shy in the classroom.

CONS:

■ Extracurricular activities can take up a lot of a teenager's time. While superior students manage to maintain good grades and also take part in extracurricular activities, average or less-than-average students often see a drop in grades during the periods of peak involvement in activities outside the classroom. Talk about this potential situation with your child *before* she or he joins after-school activities and make whatever rules or arrangements regarding homework schedules, family chores, and other responsibilities are necessary to ensure that your child can maintain her or his grade-point average as well as participation in desired activities.

■ Some extracurriculars are expensive, requiring fees, equipment, uniforms, and other costs. Financing for these activities should be a shared responsibility between you and the child. Present the financial situation to your teenager and discuss how you will help finance the activitiy and what monetary contribution you expect from her or him.

■ Participation in a school club, team, or organization can suddenly thrust a teenager into the limelight. Failure or success on the football team, in the drama club, on the debate squad, or in school politics can make special demands on a teenager's poise, confidence, and self-esteem, and she or he must be ready to deal with these demands not only within the school but sometimes within the broader community of the town or city. Discuss with your child some "what if?" scenarios: How would your child handle public competition? Success? Failure? Losing friends who are jealous or envious? Becoming jealous or envious of friends? In all discussions, tactfully guide your child to keep things in perspective—to never overvalue success, succumb too hard to failure, develop an inflated self-image, or foolishly jeopardize close relationships.

4.

Depression

Adolescence is a period when simple, moment-to-moment childhood fears are gradually replaced by more complex and lingering adult-style concerns. Like younger children, thirteen- to nineteen-year-olds continue to worry about matters of the present. In the case of adolescents, these matters include sexuality and self-image as well as social life and school performance. But unlike younger children, thirteen- to nineteen-year-olds also spend a great deal of time worrying about the future.

Some future-related concerns that bother teenagers are basically realistic in nature, such as whether and how they can get a good job, pay for college, or start a close family of their own. Other future-related concerns, however, are very idealistic in nature, such as whether and how they can find meaning in their life, purpose in their work, or peace in a world that is so politically, economically, and culturally unstable.

A teenager's vague status as a transitional being—not quite kid, not quite adult—can make any one of these worries all the more difficult to bear. Segregated from the rest of society, teenagers must continually wrestle with shifting feelings of isolation, disconnection, powerlessness, and absurdity.

Generally, adolescents are no longer raised as attentively and affectionately as they were when they were younger, which causes many of them, consciously or subconsciously, to mourn their lost childhoods or to think of themselves as neglected. At the same time, they feel pressured by their parents and society not just to grow up but to excel as individuals.

It's little wonder that an individual teenager's specific concerns, magnified by the general insecurity of adolescence, so often lead to depression. Medically, depression is an extended (two weeks or longer) episode of emotional and physical lethargy, characterized by ongoing feelings of personal worthlessness and despair. In human terms, it can mean living in purgatory, or hell itself, without any sense that things might ever change for the better.

Depression can manifest itself in many different ways, some of which may seem only dimly related, or unrelated altogether, to what people commonly associate with the word "depression." Thus, an individual case of depression may be difficult to detect.

For example, a depressed teenager may experience recurring psychosomatic symptoms, like headaches, indigestion, sleeplessness, fatigue, or rashes. For a time at least, these physical symptoms may mask the real underlying problem: emotional depression. Or a depressed teenager may resort to symptomatic behaviors, such as withdrawing from family or friends, abusing drugs, or engaging in promiscuous sex—activities that might easily and erroneously be written off as "typical acts of teenage rebelliousness."

Teenage girls suffer much higher rates of depression than teenage boys. Scientists suspect that biological factors are partly responsible (possibly relating to hormonal changes); but a great deal of the difference has to do with the culture in which we live. Females—in particular teenage females—are compelled to worry much more about personal appearance and "good" behavior than males. Moreover, their overall life expectations (the roles society casts for them and therefore the roles they envision for themselves) are far more limited. To make matters even worse, they are much more culturally conditioned than males to internalize their hostility, as opposed to discharging it on someone, or something, else.

Some scientists believe that as a result of these gender-related differences in *experiencing* depression, there are also gender-related differences in *responding* to depression. Depressed teenage boys may be more inclined to adopt "rejecting" behaviors, such as breaking off friendships, ceasing to care about schoolwork, or cursing the world, while depressed teenage girls may be more apt to adopt "self-punishing" behaviors, such as binging on food, starving themselves, or lamenting their faults and failures.

Other indicators of depression, for both teenage boys and teenage girls, include any combination of several of the following signs, extending over a period of three weeks or longer:

- a radical and otherwise inexplicable personality change of any type;
- consistently sleeping more or less than usual;
- repeated attempts to run away;
- frequent and lengthy bouts of anger or violent behavior;
- chronic boredom;
- ongoing inability to concentrate, pay attention, or think clearly;
- loss of interest in activities formerly enjoyed;

■ persistent lack of tolerance for compliments or rewards;

■ continual and pronounced pessimism about the future;

■ repeated and uncharacteristic episodes of crying or tearfulness;

■ increasing tendency toward lying, thoughtlessness, carelessness, or sloppiness.

Parents of depressed teenagers are frequently advised by well-meaning friends or family members to ignore their child's depression; but, in fact, this is bad advice. Although few interpersonal activities are more challenging than communicating with a teenager who is stuck in a negative rut, her or his parents should make every reasonable effort to do so. It is precisely because teenagers are so capable of becoming stuck in a negative rut that they need all the help they can get. Parents of teenagers must never forget that teenage depression in its most extreme form can be literally a matter of life and death.

Whenever your teenage child seems depressed, try following these guidelines:

■ Be especially loving and supportive.

Remember that teenagers often feel that their parents don't love them as warmly or as much as when they were younger and "cuter." During a period of depression, this feeling can be painfully acute—whether or not there is a basis for it in reality.

Try returning in spirit to the time when your depressed child was much younger. Demonstrate your love and support in some of the same ways that used to please her or him then, modified slightly to suit her or his present age. For example, increase the number of times that you touch your child affectionately, make praising reference to her or his good qualities, or simply "goof around." The goal is not necessarily to "baby" your child but to ensure that you don't inadvertently give your child any reason to doubt that you care.

■ Take the initiative in talking with your child.

Don't wait anxiously for your depressed child to come to you. Show your concern about the symptoms you've noticed and indicate your desire to talk about whatever might be bothering her or him.

It is certainly appropriate to give your depressed child *some* time and space to be alone and quiet. However, it doesn't make sense to leave your child entirely on her or his own, expecting her or him to take the lead in communicating with you or even to meet you halfway. A depressed person—teenage or not—can easily be incapable of making such gestures. It's up to you, as the more emotionally stable person, to coax your child into opening up.

■ *Help your child think constructively instead of destructively.*
A depressed person is inclined to see only the darkest aspects of a situation. The best way to help such a person conquer depression is to assist her or him in seeing brighter possibilities.

Suppose, for example, that your depressed child insists on maintaining a discouragingly single-minded and extremist point of view, making statements like "There's nothing I can do about it," "I always wind up making a mess of things," or "There's only one thing that can happen." In a tactful but persistent manner, point out that there are indeed positive alternatives that she or he is overlooking.

In other words, get your child to *start* thinking about various ways to get out of the rut of depression and to *stop* thinking merely about the rut itself. Don't expect an instant, positive response to your efforts. Your child may even fight against you temporarily. But the overall effect will be to restimulate her or his healthy imagination.

■ *Guide your child toward activities that are creative or self-affirming.*
Try to interest your depressed child in some form of artistic self-expression. Often depressed people can cure themselves by discharging their emotional strife into paintings, poems, sculptures, compositions, songs, dances, or crafts.

Another way for a person to dispel her or his depression is to become involved in helping others. Search for possible volunteer groups, community service activities, or social service programs that might be appropriate for your child and encourage her or him (perhaps by joining in yourself) to take part in one or more of them.

Finally, identify your depressed child's personal talents (e.g., in athletics or science) and social strengths (e.g., in teaching or teamwork) and then steer her or him toward activities in which these talents and strengths can be exercised. You'll be helping your child rebuild self-esteem and in the process recover her or his good spirits.

■ *Teach your child how to relax.*
Many depressed individuals simply don't know how to comfort themselves or put themselves in a better, more congenial frame of mind. Let your child know what you yourself do to relax by yourself, especially if it's something simple and easy to appreciate, like walking in a nearby park, shooting baskets, sketching outdoor scenes, or taking a long, hot bath.

You might also try researching several of the more popular and effective formal relaxation techniques: for example, deep breathing, visualization, meditation, or yoga. Gather information at your local library, health club, or stress-reduction center. Then either share what you learn directly with your child or arrange for your child (and perhaps yourself as well) to be instructed by a qualified teacher.

■ *Provide diversionary entertainments.*

As much as is practical, set up fun things for your child, you and your child together, and the whole family to do. For example, arrange a video night, a picnic, a boat trip, a visit to an amusement park, or a night out at a roller rink. The more novel the entertainment, the more likely it is to jolt your child out of her or his depression.

In trying to show your depressed child a good time, guard against making her or him too self-conscious about your intentions or expecting her or him to respond at the time in a positive or even noticeable manner. The good effects of the experience may be slow to reveal themselves. On the other hand, your child may continue to be— or appear—just as depressed as ever.

The most important point of providing diversionary entertainments is not to let your child wallow in uninterrupted gloom; rather, to give fun every possible chance. If at first you don't succeed, keep on trying.

■ *Do whatever you reasonably can to reduce stress at home.*

In many cases, one of the main factors contributing to a teenager's depression is stress at home. Common stressors of this type include marital discord, separation, or divorce; fighting between siblings; overcrowding; a serious illness, misfortune, or death suffered by a family member; economic insecurity; a recent or impending move; or simple disorganization: a lack of comforting order and dependable routines.

Even in cases of teenage depression when stress at home is *not* one of the main initiating factors, it definitely deepens the depression and makes it last longer. No matter how unrelated the stress at home may originally be to the teenager's depression, she or he will ultimately come to feel personally responsible for that stress. From the distorted and egocentric point of view of a typical depressed teenager, she or he is a psychic stress generator or stress magnet that can't help but cause trouble for everyone else.

For some depressed teenagers, this "irrational" sense of responsibility leads to overwhelming guilt and shame, which, in turn, renders them exceedingly passive. For others, it leads to resentment and rebellion. Unable to tolerate feeling personally guilty or ashamed, they actively project blame onto everyone around them. In either scenario, the sad consequence can be not only a self-destructing individual life but also a ruined family life.

To help your depressed teenager and your family avoid such crises, make every effort to keep family life running smoothly; for example:

■ Maintain a structure of regular mealtimes, playtimes, and work times that everyone can rely on.

■ Avoid any dramatic household disruptions, such as putting up guests for a week or conducting major renovations.

■ See to it that everyone respects each other's rights, including some degree of privacy.

■ Build opportunities into each day for rewarding person-to-person contact not only with your depressed teenager but also with other members of your family, who, during such a crisis, are also in need of special love and understanding.

■ *Consider seeking professional help.*

A teenager's depression is never something to take lightly. While it lasts, it can wreak havoc on her or his personal, family, social, and school life. And at its most extreme, it can result in seriously abusive behavior and even suicide.

If repeated attempts to rouse your teenage child from depression have had no success after several weeks and if you are worried that the depression may, in fact, be getting worse, think about getting professional help. Psychological treatment can be very effective in helping teenagers overcome their depression. And there is also the medical angle. Many cases of depression—especially severe depression—have biochemical causes that can be greatly alleviated with medication. By taking quick, responsible action to investigate the psychological and medical aspects of your child's depression, you may be sparing yourself, your child, and your family months and even years of turmoil and grief.

At PCGC:
The Onset of Adulthood

Adolescence is an awkward time from start to finish, but the years between ages seventeen and twenty-one—when an individual isn't so much a "teenager" as a "young person"—can be particularly difficult. For some individuals, the sheer accumulation of new responsibilities, demands, freedoms, and constraints that are associated with this final period of transition to adulthood can be unbearable.

Caught in a downward spiral of self-doubt, self-defeat, and

self-destructiveness, these particularly traumatized individuals may exhibit several signs of severe depression:

- extreme moodiness;

- recurring thoughts of death and/or suicide;

- frequent displays of temper;

- long periods of withdrawal;

- intense substance abuse;

- sexual promiscuity and/or abuse;

- eating disorders;

- chronic health or hygiene problems.

In such cases, professional intervention may well be required if the downward spiral is ever to be reversed. And the sooner the intervention occurs, the better.

Increasingly, hospitals and clinics are providing therapeutic programs to deal with the special needs of troubled adolescents and their families. The goal of such programs is to identify the problem *quickly* and initiate *rapid* change. They help the young person alter self-defeating behaviors, reestablish productive relationships within the family, and develop the emotional resources and coping skills needed to succeed as an adult. At the same time, other members of the young person's family are frequently assisted in resolving their interpersonal conflicts and in building stronger relationships with one another so that the family as a whole can provide a supportive context for the young person's renewed growth as an emotionally healthy human being.

PCGC offers a program of this type called the Transitions Program. The success of the Transitions Program has been guided by the philosophy that each patient presents a unique combination of strengths and weaknesses, difficulties and capabilities, needs and opportunities. The program's focus is to help each patient make the most of this combination, that is, to capitalize on her or his strengths and capabilities, to effect positive change in her or his difficulties and weaknesses, and to fulfill her or his needs and opportunities.

A patient in the Transitions Program always benefits from talking privately with an understanding professional. However, our experience supports the fact that the entire family working together can provide additional and unparalleled assistance to the young person in her or his efforts toward achieving independence and assuming a valued new role in the family as an adult. For this reason, the family as a whole usually participates in the intervention.

The first step in the Transitions Program is a general assessment of the young person's life situation and emotional well-being. It's made to help us understand the young person in the context of her or his family, school, peers, and community. A detailed treatment plan is then developed, which is typically implemented on an outpatient basis, and may include any—or all—of the following components:

■ specialized psychological, psychiatric, and/or neurological evaluations;

■ individual therapy;

■ family therapy;

■ psychopharmacological therapy (i.e., therapy involving medications);

■ psychoeducational counseling for the patient and family.

These outpatient services are offered through the Professional Services Group, Inc., the private practice affiliate of PCGC. Locations include PCGC's main facility in University City, Philadelphia, and satellite locations throughout suburban Philadelphia and southern New Jersey.

In the more serious diagnostic or treatment conditions, inpatient hospitalization may be indicated. Given such a case, a multidisciplinary team, in consultation with the family and referring therapist(s), develops a specific treatment plan to stabilize the crisis at hand and to meet the immediate, most pressing needs of the patient and her or his family. The plan includes specific short-term goals and tasks to help the young person and her or his family disrupt self-defeating patterns and achieve rapid and positive change. Thereafter, for as long a period of time as necessary, the plan is repeatedly reviewed with the patient and her or his family so that it can be revised as appropriate.

If your child, or a child you know, seems to be suffering serious emotional problems in making the transition from adolescence to adulthood, this type of program—or therapeutic approach—may be very helpful. Contact local mental-health authorities for information and guidance.

Preventing Teenage Suicide

Suicide is the most drastic manifestation of depression; among American teenagers, it is the third leading cause of death. In a 1991 Gallup poll, 6 percent of the teenagers interviewed admitted to having attempted suicide at least once in their lives, and 15 percent said they had "come very close to trying."

These percentages may not seem large in themselves, but they are appalling when one considers the age of the victims and how desperate they must have been to try to end their lives so prematurely.

To the tormented adolescent psyche, still so vulnerable to stress, self-doubt, pessimism, grief, and hopelessness, suicide can appear to be a very compelling means of escaping pain. Indeed, it can sometimes seem to be the ideal, perhaps the only, solution to the problem at hand: for example, what to do after a love affair has ended, how to end the messy conflicts surrounding the divorce of one's parents, what to do with an unwanted body or mind, or how to deal with the threat of possible annihilation in a nuclear war or ecological disaster. In situations like these, a teenager can feel especially powerless, lacking either the ability to change or the coping skills to deal with what's happening. To teenagers who feel this way, the act of suicide can appear to be the only powerful act they're capable of performing.

Depressed teenagers are also highly susceptible to contemplating or committing suicide after learning that a peer has done so. Thus, the suicide of one teenager is sometimes quickly followed by the suicides of other teenagers in her or his community.

Known scientifically as the "cluster effect," this phenomenon of one teenage suicide prompting others offers yet one more example of an adolescent's tendency to identify so strongly with her or his peers and to react so emotionally to what they say and do. Having been swept away by the drama of another teenager's suicide, a depressed adolescent may be all the more likely to view it as a possible and even glamorous alternative to her or his present, miserable existence.

The danger signals of suicidal feelings are similar to those of depression, with the possible addition of any one or more of the following behaviors:

■ complaining about being "rotten inside" or "dying" (e.g., "I feel like I'm going to die");

■ expressing verbal hints, such as "You won't have to worry about me much longer" or "I can't put up with feeling this way anymore";

■ putting her or his affairs in order, for example, by giving away possessions, ending relationships, cleaning her or his room especially well;

■ becoming suddenly and inexplicably composed or cheerful after a long period of depression;

■ making secret arrangements for some sort of atypical outing or private ceremony.

The most effective step that concerned parents can take to prevent their depressed teenager from committing suicide is to be extra vigilant. People who are thinking about suicide almost always give clues, intentionally or unintentionally; and this type of clue giving is especially prevalent among teenagers. Whenever such a clue appears, parents should take it very seriously and intervene as quickly as possible.

Here are some guidelines for intervening effectively to prevent your teenager from contemplating, attempting, or committing suicide:

■ *Ask your child if she or he is depressed or thinking of suicide.*

It may be awkward to bring up these subjects or talk about them once they are out in the open, but there's nothing to lose and everything to gain. Your child may be too inhibited in general or too immersed in her or his specific problems to confide in you without some prompting.

Don't hesitate to confront your child with these matters out of a fear that you will be putting negative or dangerous ideas into her or his head. Suicidal ideation (the formal term for "seriously thinking along suicidal lines") is not provoked in this way. Instead, you will be letting your child appreciate how much you care, rescuing her or him from any self-imposed spell of secrecy, and making it easier for him or her to be frank with you.

■ *Work with your child to find constructive solutions to her or his suicide-related problems.*

With tact and compassion, suggest ways that your child might go about addressing her or his suicide-related problems both with and without your help. Encourage your child to talk about possible problem solutions with specific individuals whom you trust—people who will be discreet, patient, supportive, and upbeat and who don't necessarily need to know that your child has been, or may be, contemplating suicide.

■ *Talk with your child about local teenage suicides that come to your attention.*

The more that the two of you discuss such suicides up front, the less chance that your child will fantasize about them, take them too much to heart, or imitate them in a "cluster effect" reaction. Together with your child, talk realistically and in detail about what circumstances and feelings may have led up to that particular suicide, what more constructive actions the victim might have taken, and what effects the suicide may be having on the victim's friends and family members as well as on strangers hearing about it.

■ *Set and enforce rules and routines that will give your child's daily life a healthy structure.*

Arrange your family's day-to-day home life so that it is more predictable, less stressful, and less conducive to providing your child with incentives or opportunities to engage in suicidal thoughts or activities. Taking care to elicit and honor any wishes your child may have regarding confidentiality, involve all family members in planning these arrangements.

Avoid making changes that are too extreme or abrupt or that appear too obviously related to your child's confessed inclination toward suicide. Otherwise, you might make your child feel punished or confined. But *do* make changes that will encourage your child, yourself, and others of your family to act more responsibly and considerately toward each other.

Among the policies to consider instituting or reinforcing are the following:

■ making sure that family members keep each other informed about their daily schedules;

■ setting up regular and peaceful times when family members are expected to be together (e.g., at supper) as well as regular and peaceful times that you and your depressed child can be together;

■ not leaving your depressed child (or any other child in the family) alone for extended periods of time without adult supervision;

■ establishing a strict curfew at night for all children and a limited number of nights per week when they can be away from home;

■ not permitting your children to tease, provoke attack, or otherwise bother each other and not allowing any such incident to pass by unmentioned.

■ *Get professional help.*

Severe depression and suicidal ideation are serious mental disorders. They are also treatable. If you have any reason to believe that your child is suffering from these disorders, then arrange to have her or him evaluated by a psychiatrist, psychologist, or mental-health professional.

A psychological evaluation will not obligate your child to enter a treatment program, nor will it have an adverse impact on your child's emotional well-being. On the contrary, it can help both of you face your child's emotional problems more directly and intelligently, and it provides both of you with an invaluable contact and resource in the event of a future crisis.

CASE:

The Double Deal

Ed remembered the event vividly as "the worst night in my life." It had happened three months ago, shortly after his fifteenth birthday. His parents had gone out in his father's car for dinner at a friend's house. On a very uncharacteristic impulse, he had decided to take a short, forbidden, and illegal drive in his mother's car, not only just for the fun of it but also to get some practice driving so that he wouldn't look so amateurish when the "formal" lessons with his father began.

As luck would have it, Ed drove right past his parents, who were returning home unexpectedly. Stepping on the gas to get away before they could see him, he jumped the curb and drove onto someone's lawn. As soon as he got back onto the street, his father pulled in behind him.

Understandably torn by anger, fear, disappointment, and disbelief, Ed's father yelled at him for risking his life, stealing the car, and digging up the lawn. Then, shaking his head over his otherwise mild-mannered, law-abiding son's bad luck at being caught, his father exclaimed, "You're such a loser!"

Thereafter, both Ed and his father appeared to have put the incident behind them. But Ed gradually spent less and less time with the family and more and more time alone in his room listening to music with his headphones on. Since he wasn't causing any noticeable problems, his parents just decided to let him be. He was eating much less, but then he had needed to lose weight, anyway. A month after the car-stealing incident, his report card showed a significant drop in his grades, so his parents applied more pressure on him to do his homework and hoped for the best.

Finally, three weeks later, something happened that Ed's parents couldn't excuse or ignore: They caught him smoking marijuana in his bedroom. An immediate search of his bedroom revealed several ounces of marijuana and a half-empty bottle of scotch. Concerned that their otherwise quiet, solitary, and well-behaved child might get into serious trouble by using drugs, they sought family counseling.

The counselor supported Ed's parents' drug-prohibition policy: Drugs and drug use were *not* to be permitted in the house; and any evidence or reasonable suspicion that drugs *were* in the house or that drug use *was* taking place would warrant a full search. But more important, the counselor enabled Ed and his parents to see that the problem was not the drugs per se but an underlying depression.

Ed had been devastated by hearing his father call him "a loser" on the night he had stolen his mother's car. That one remark had brought to the surface all the feelings of foolishness, incompetence, worthlessness, and hopelessness that he had been suppressing since puberty, when the awkward process of going through adolescence had begun. During the weeks that had followed his father's remark, he had not been able to rid his mind of those feelings. All he could do was occasionally drown them out with music and drugs.

Working with the counselor, Ed came to understand that he needed to confront his parents about things they did that upset him rather than simply brooding about them. As it turned out, Ed's father had completely forgotten the offending remark and had certainly not meant it as seriously as his son had taken it. Ed's father also said that he had felt for some time like sitting down with his son and asking him why he had been so withdrawn lately—something the counselor agreed would have been a good thing to do—but that he had been too embarrassed or afraid to do so.

Moved by the knowledge that his father, too, suffered from

embarrassment and fear, Ed was more willing to admit his own role in letting himself become so depressed. He grew to appreciate that his father couldn't turn him into a loser just by saying he was. Only Ed himself could do that. And with his newfound appreciation came a resolve never to let that happen.

After the counseling, two deals were made. Ed and his parents struck a bargain with each other that whenever a conflict arose, everyone involved would discuss it as soon as they were calm in order to eliminate misunderstandings and resolve hurt feelings. And Ed struck a bargain with himself that he would not blame someone else for getting him down as long as it was in his power to pick himself back up.

At PCGC: Seasonal Affective Disorder

Seasonal affective disorder, or SAD, is a form of depression that appears to be related to seasonal changes in natural light, as registered on the retina and processed in the brain. Other factors that may trigger SAD are wintertime temperature and humidity changes. SAD may also be experienced in summer instead of winter, a condition called reverse SAD. This latter condition, far less prevalent than SAD itself, may be caused by a latent summer-hibernation drive in the victim's brain, like the one that is activated in many animals during hot and dry seasons. In either case—SAD or reverse SAD—the symptoms are similar: decreased alertness, increased sleepiness, and sustained lack of enthusiasm for life.

The Mood, Sleep, and Seasonality Program at PCGC studies how child and adolescent depression relates to the seasons and what long-term effects such depression may have on its sufferers. The program has established that adolescents with SAD regularly exhibit various combinations of the following symptoms during the winter months:

■ extreme tiredness and listlessness;

■ appetite changes: most often an *increase* in appetite (possibly as the result of winter-triggered carbohydrate-craving obesity syndrome [COS]);

■ recurring general complaints of "not feeling well";

■ frequent irritability, negativity, and impatience;

■ persistent and pronounced sadness;

■ difficulty in concentrating, often accompanied by a slowness in thinking and causing a downward trend in school performance;

■ sleep changes: either too much or too little;

■ withdrawal from family and peer social activities.

According to what the Mood, Sleep, and Seasonality Program has learned to date, adolescent SAD is less severe than adult SAD but more severe than cases of school-age SAD. The implication is that an untreated case of SAD worsens over time and that early intervention can make a significant difference in the victim's lifelong emotional state.

An adolescent is referred to PCGC's Mood, Sleep, and Seasonality Program by her or his parents and/or teachers. A psychiatrist then assesses the various biological, psychological, environmental, and family elements that may be contributing to the adolescent's apparently season-related depression. One such element may be heredity. Both SAD and other forms of extreme seasonal mood and energy variation tend to occur in family groups; and family members from different generations may go through persistent seasonal mood changes of differing intensities.

Ultimately, the program psychiatrist arrives at a specific diagnosis, which may point to season-related depression but not SAD itself. Then the psychiatrist outlines a treatment plan tailored to the particular needs of the adolescent and her or his family.

Among the most successful treatments for SAD is phototherapy, which involves daily exposure for approximately an hour or more (depending on the case) to banks of high-intensity light. This type of exposure has worked to counteract many of the effects of SAD in approximately 80 percent of the patients admitted to the program.

If you think your child, or a child you know, may be suffering from SAD, consult your psychiatrist, psychologist, or mental-health professional. He or she can help you arrange for diagnosis and (if necessary) treatment.

5.

Discipline

Among all the tasks associated with raising children, disciplining a teenager typically causes the greatest amount of emotional wear and tear for parent and child alike. In fact, it is the complexity of this task and not really the nature of being a teenager in itself that gives adolescence its bad reputation of being such a disturbing and turbulent developmental period.

Once adolescence begins, parents can no longer rely so much on their superior physical, social, and intellectual status to compel obedience to their authority. Instead, their teenage children are increasingly capable of seeing through that authority and challenging it. And no longer are adolescents so attached to small pleasures, like dessert and a night's worth of television, or so terrified by small pains, like having to stay in their room for a few hours. Instead, they are increasingly more interested in waging and winning power struggles over their long-range rights and liberties.

The upshot is that parents have less and less control over their teenage child as she or he gets older and older. This process is inevitable no matter what approach to discipline parents may take. It is also, in essence, appropriate and desirable. Adolescents need to learn how to control themselves rather than depending on their parents to perform that function for them. Otherwise, they will be at a serious disadvantage when they eventually leave home and are obliged to make their own way in life.

Understandably, parents of teenagers find it very difficult to yield their hard-won child-governing powers or to stand by helplessly as they lose them. Their loss of power is even harder to accept given the dangers that individual teenagers can encounter or create for themselves during their quest for independence.

Wrestling with this dilemma, parents often subconsciously turn situations that seem to call for disciplinary measures into opportunities to discharge their personal anger, frustration, and fear. Ultimately, this strategy is as futile as it is unfair. Having lost their composure, parents wind up even more upset; and having been subject to such raw antagonism, their children wind up even more alienated and therefore uncooperative.

Meanwhile, teenagers are not nearly as strong-willed or ready for self-determination as they may *appear* to be. Nor are they always capable of seeing the lack of logic or the inconsistencies that exist in their thoughts and behaviors. Their strong degree of self-absorption frequently renders them blind to their faults and mistakes no matter how apparent they may be to a parent or how well a parent may describe them and point them out.

Many parent-child disciplinary struggles that occur during a child's teenage years are triggered by deep conflicts that are common within the adolescent psyche. While teenagers may consciously believe that they want to break away from their parents, subconsciously they still desire a certain amount of parental attention, concern, and guidance. And while they may consciously think they are old enough to be treated as adults, subconsciously they know that they are not sufficiently mature in emotional or intellectual terms to appreciate many of the values and responsibilities that adult life entails.

Taking into account this fragile balance within the adolescent ego, parents must discipline their teenage children with extreme caution. They must be careful not to alienate their children by appearing to "baby" them. At the same time, they must not only give their children a clear and palpable sense of how they are expected to behave but also help them accept and meet those behavioral standards.

To discipline your thirteen- to nineteen-year-old child with a maximum of constructive guidance and a minimum of destructive stress, try following these basic recommendations:

■ *Always strive to educate rather than to dictate.*

Your primary disciplinary objective is to influence your teenage child toward becoming more self-disciplined. After all, it won't be long before she or he will be outside the pale of your day-to-day support and authority.

With this in mind, make every effort to appeal to your child's reason and common sense. Involve her or him in negotiating rules. Check to be sure that she or he understands the rationale behind requests and policies that affect her or his life-style and behavior. Avoid issuing commands in a spirit of "do it because I say so."

In other words, as your teenager grows up, treat her or him more and more like an adult and less and less like a child. Build on your successes in this endeavor and involve your child in seeking alternatives to strategies that clearly aren't working.

■ *Accept as much as possible in your child's behavior, even if you can't approve.*

Because of their rapidly changing physical, emotional, and social lives and their increasing desire and need to exercise their independence, teenagers are bound to behave more erratically and generate more potential conflict than they did as younger children. This calls for a more tolerant and judicious response on the part of parents. Requiring your teenager to conform to household rules and family standards just as much as she or he used to do is only inviting an ever-increasing degree of friction and hostility at home.

Reserve disciplinary actions for situations that are truly serious, that is, situations in which your child has interfered with someone else's rights, has caused harm to someone else's person or property, or has placed someone else's welfare in jeopardy. The same goes for criticisms and complaints, which, to a thin-skinned teenager, can seem just as harsh and insulting as disciplinary action.

This approach means being careful in the first place not to set up too many rules, regulations, and guidelines governing your teenager's behavior. Otherwise, you put your teenager at risk of repeatedly doing something offensive and yourself at risk of repeatedly having to express your displeasure with your child—or else lose your credibility as a parent. Keep official rules to the bare minimum and give your child as much freedom as practical to learn from her or his own mistakes.

■ *Be firm and consistent in administering discipline.*

Although it may not be apparent on the surface, your teenager depends on you to establish and uphold *some* degree of order in her or his life. Stand behind whatever disciplinary rules and policies you do set up with your teenager, such as curfews, reporting procedures, or household chores. Never ignore a violation and try not to be noticeably inconsistent in addressing it—treating the same degree of violation very lightly on one occasion and very harshly on another. Instead, try to address each violation with approximately equal seriousness.

In addition, strive to maintain control over every phase of the disciplinary process. Of course, it is appropriate and desirable to negotiate rules with your teenage child rather than simply imposing your own rules. It is also appropriate and desirable to listen to what your teenager has to say about any violations that occur rather than simply leveling accusations and judgments. However, set a reasonable limit to such open-ended discussions. Your word should be the final one.

■ *Try not to get emotionally involved or upset during disciplinary confrontations.*

In the heat of an argument, an angry or frustrated teenager is likely to say all sorts of things that are capable of hurting your feelings. Don't take such statements too much to heart; rather, recognize them for what they are: desperate and, more often than not, thoughtless attempts to throw you off balance.

Alternatively, guard against getting carried away yourself and saying things that you don't want or mean to say. If you feel yourself becoming too angry or frustrated to continue a particular confrontation wisely and compassionately, then discontinue the confrontation, setting up a specific time in the near future (preferably that same day) to discuss the matter more calmly.

At all times, remember that your objective is to get your child to *behave* well, not to force her or him to have the same *feelings* as you about a particular incident or rule. Your child may not have the privilege of acting in whatever way she or he pleases but does have a right to her or his own personal opinions and attitudes.

■ *Avoid administering specific punishments unless absolutely necessary.*

Punishments for a teenage child do not have the same effect as they do for a preschooler or school-age child. A teenager is much less likely to be intimidated or reformed by having to do a particular penance for some transgression.

Nor is punishment of a teenager as easy to devise and enforce. The most common forms of teenage punishment are grounding, the imposition of special chores, or the reduction of certain privileges (e.g., using the family car, talking on the telephone, or watching television). A teenager is not only more capable of tolerating or working around such temporary inconveniences but also more capable of defying them.

Never forget that a teenager is determined to be treated as an adult and therefore frequently responds as one. This means that a well-managed disciplinary criticism or confrontation in itself may often turn out to be a sufficiently effective form of punishment.

Whenever it seems necessary to discipline your teenage child, try limiting yourself at first to confrontation and constructive criticism. Only resort to a specific punishment if the initial tactic fails to prevent repetition of the same wrongdoing.

Experiment with asking your misbehaving teenager what punishment would be appropriate, given the situation at hand. Your teenager may be harder on her- or himself than you would or could be. Besides, your teenager will have no legitimate grounds for complaining that the punishment is unfair if she or he actually determines it.

■ *Don't embarrass or humiliate your child.*
Teenagers have a great deal of pride. They can be very easily and severely wounded by sharp, punishing references to their inadequacies, vulnerabilities, and mistakes, however warranted you may feel such references are. And once wounded in this manner, teenagers usually become even more resentful, obstinate, and prone to bad behavior.

As much as possible, spare your child's feelings. Focus on what is wrong with the *act* your child has committed rather than on what is wrong with her or him. Give your child reason to believe that she or he is capable of behaving better and express your faith that she or he *will* behave better.

■ *Set a good example.*
Your child can't be expected to abide by rules for good behavior if you don't. Furthermore, your child can't be expected to know how to manage self-discipline in general if she or he can't look to you as a model.

Exercise self-control and respect for others in your personal habits. Live up to your side of any bargain that you strike with your child— or any bargain that your child knows you have struck. Obey all rules that apply to the family in general (e.g., reporting whereabouts, showing up for meals, keeping common spaces tidy, not disturbing each other's privacy). And do your best to obey all rules that apply to society in general.

■ *Recognize when matters have worsened beyond your ability to cope and seek appropriate help.*
You should never be ashamed to admit your helplessness in dealing with a particular teenage discipline problem or with your teenager's disciplinary problems in general. The potential price of not admitting your helplessness is the emotional well-being of every member of your family as well as those individuals outside your family who are heavily influenced by your teenager's behavior.

In any of the following situations, consider contacting a psychiatrist, a psychologist, a mental-health professional, or any adult whose judgment you respect and whose experience seems applicable:

> ■ Your child persists in ignoring or violating all household rules and policies.

> ■ You are unable to maintain control of your own behavior in confrontations with your child.

■ Your child is suffering from severe depression, perhaps even having suicidal thoughts.

■ Your child is developing serious health problems, such as poor eating or sleeping habits.

■ Your child shows signs of being addicted to a drug.

■ Your child appears unable to stop tormenting or abusing another child, either inside or outside the family.

■ Your child's school performance is irreversibly deteriorating.

■ Your child is unable to break a pattern of consistent lying or stealing.

■ Your child is repeatedly absent from home or truant from school for long periods of time without explanation.

■ You are often—or persistently—afraid of your child.

■ You realize your child has a serious problem of some sort, but you can't identify it.

CASE:

A Lesson in Responsibility

Marsha was a stable and trustworthy sixteen-year-old with a streak of wildness. Her classmate Kate, on the other hand, was basically wild—too wild for Marsha ever to let her mother, Phyllis, meet her or even know that they sometimes hung out together.

One weekend afternoon while Phyllis was away, Marsha invited Kate over to her house. Phyllis returned just as Kate's car was pulling out of the driveway. An hour later, Phyllis discovered that fifty dollars was missing from her top bureau drawer.

Without making any direct accusations, Phyllis informed Marsha that she had placed the fifty dollars in her drawer just before she had gone out that afternoon and asked Marsha if she knew anything about its disappearance. At first, Marsha denied that she or Kate had any knowledge of what might have happened to it. But when Phyllis finally stated that she had no reasonable alternative but to believe that either Marsha or Kate had taken the money, Marsha admitted that Kate had wandered freely throughout the house and might have taken the money.

Phyllis refrained from scolding her daughter. Instead, she stated clearly and firmly that she held Marsha responsible for the theft and in the future would continue to hold her responsible for whatever might happen inside the house while she was home alone and in charge. Then Phyllis secured Marsha's agreement to repay the money personally. Finally, Phyllis established a new policy: If Marsha ever again let someone who was a stranger to Phyllis into the house while she was away, Phyllis would feel compelled to make sure that Marsha was not left home alone thereafter.

Marsha was appreciative of the fact that Phyllis didn't blame her for inviting Kate into the house in the first place— or even for associating with Kate—something Marsha no longer felt inclined to do, anyway. She was also grateful that she was still trusted at home alone. And she had no trouble accepting the new policy of no strangers in the house. After all, she might not be able to afford them!

Authoritarian-Restrictive Versus Authoritative

In all dealings with your teenage child, it is helpful to bear in mind the distinction between an *authoritarian-restrictive* parenting style and an *authoritative* parenting style. The latter style tends to be far more productive and satisfying than the former style from both the parents' perspective and that of the child.

An authoritarian-restrictive parent is one whose disciplinary efforts mainly involve negative-oriented behaviors: saying "No!" or "Wrong," setting rules and limits to curb "bad" behavior, and administering punishment. On the other hand, an authoritative parent is one whose disciplinary efforts mainly involve positive-oriented behaviors: saying "Yes!" or "Right," setting a good example, and administering praise for "good" behavior.

In essence, an authoritarian-restrictive parent inspires fear and resentment in a child; an authoritative parent, love and respect. You may not always be able to avoid making your child afraid of you or to keep your child from resenting you. But you can prevent yourself from drifting into the habit of disciplining your child in a manner that is *primarily* negative.

Concentrate on phrasing disciplinary measures in terms of what is good or right to do (and why) instead of what your child is *not* allowed to do. Scrupulously practice the behavior that you want emulated and make it a point to compliment far more often than you correct your child.

6.

Divorce

Divorce is always traumatic for every family member. Adolescent children are no exception. Despite any mask of self-possession, coolheadedness, or aloofness that teenagers may present to the outside world, their inner emotional lives are full of dramatic ups and downs. This turbulence inevitably worsens as they react to the growing emotional needs of their divorcing parents, especially if the children think—rightly or wrongly—that their parents are putting pressure upon them to take sides in the issues surrounding the divorce.

The individual teenager may instinctively hide her or his true feelings about a parental breakup, but these feelings don't simply stay quiet or go away. Somehow they manifest themselves. They may trigger short-term, intensified problems with schoolwork or with siblings. Even long after the divorce, they may be the underlying cause of low self-esteem and troubled relationships with schoolmates, teachers, and, most especially, would-be or actual romantic partners.

If you are contemplating or going through a divorce, consider these ways to prevent, alleviate, or resolve the tensions that your adolescent child may experience:

■ *Be sensitive to your teenage child's need for information, emotional equilibrium, and a personal sense of safety throughout the divorce period.*

As the divorce approaches, don't put your teenager on the spot by involving her or him in divorce-related decisions. Avoid criticizing or casting blame upon your partner in your child's presence, as this will only put her or him on the defensive. Keep your child informed about divorce-related events and the decisions that you have *already* made in a timely and frank manner. And, as much as possible, avoid making radical changes in your child's normal routines (such as a change of home, a change of school, or a major trip) until at least a few months after the divorce is final.

■ *Bear in mind that adolescents usually expect their parents to take every possible step to avoid divorce, so they need to be convinced that the divorce decision is a valid and final one.*

Losing a parent through a divorce is one of the worst fears a child can have at any age. Most adolescents believe (or want to believe) that any problem can be resolved by adults if they make sufficient efforts to do so. Teenage children will expect their parents, especially, to live up to their responsibility of being mature, rational, and responsible adults. For an adolescent to accept what will appear as his or her parents' "failure" to resolve their differences, the parents will have to explain very conclusively that all other *reasonable* alternatives have been considered and that no other recourse is possible.

■ *Assure your child that she or he is not at fault in causing the divorce.*

In addition to convincing your teenage child that you have given due consideration to every possible solution to save your marriage, it is important to communicate that she or he is not to blame for your inability to stay together. Reassure your child that the divorce-related problems are strictly between you and your partner, and that your child does not have to choose sides or come to any decision about which of you is more at fault.

Teenagers have a passion for knowing the truth. Therefore, your adolescent child needs to hear from you clearly and unambiguously that she or he did not create irreconcilable differences between you and your partner. Also, reassure your child that both you and your partner will still love her or him just as much after you've divorced.

■ *Be ready for the fact your teenager may see the divorce as "good."*

Although divorce is always painful, a surprising number of adolescents have little trouble believing that an impending divorce will be "good" for their parents. In most cases of stormy or failing marriages, the teenage children are keenly aware of the problems their parents are having—and of how those problems are impinging negatively on their own teenage lives! In many of such cases, the children respond to the actual breakup of their parents with a sense of relief and even optimism.

For example, an adolescent daughter may sympathize with a mother who is being abused by her partner—even though her mother's partner is her own beloved father—and may recognize that a divorce will bring an end to a painful period of victimization. A teenage boy may appreciate a father's need to break free from a partner who is relentlessly critical, manipulative, and nonsupportive, thereby preventing him from reaching his goals. A teenage child of either gender may see why one parent's infidelity makes it impossible for the other parent to continue the marriage.

The fact that adolescents can envision positive reasons for a divorce, however, does not mean that they are free from the disruption it causes in their personal lives, nor does it prevent them from possibly experiencing occasional periods of anger, resentment, guilt, and hostility— even against their will. While you need to accept a teenage child's professed judgment that the divorce is "good" or "understandable," you need to accept at the same time that the child may still need help coping with troublesome divorce-related emotions. When she or he is upset, try to avoid merely appealing to logic by saying something like, "I thought you understood why we needed to get divorced." Instead, be comforting and supportive.

■ Don't use your teenager as a scapegoat for your own divorce-related emotions.

Immediately after the divorce, you may still need to express your anger and resentment toward your ex-husband or ex-wife. Be careful not to indulge in angry outbursts toward your teenage children during this period, however tempted you may be. The situation can quickly get out of hand. Since adolescents are naturally inclined to test parental limits as part of their growing-up process, it is easy for their parents to attack them *personally* whenever they overstep the bounds, rather than simply to discipline them, as they would a younger child.

It is important to recognize the extra degree of emotional turmoil that your teenager is going through because of the divorce. Always take care not to use your child, consciously or unconsciously, as a scapegoat for negative feelings that you still harbor for your ex-partner. If anything, you may need to be a little more tolerant of your child's shortcomings and failings in the months immediately after the divorce, giving her or him the benefit of the doubt whenever possible, rather than risk losing your temper disproportionately over minor infractions.

■ Try to arrange responsibilities so that both you and your ex-partner function as parents.

Children suffer less from a divorce when both parents continue to function in their lives *as parents*. While one ex-partner is usually granted custody of the child, the other ex-partner should continue to remain a vital and nurturing force in the child's world: superintending his or her behavior, guiding his or her mental and emotional development, and performing a certain number of the chores associated with raising a teenage child.

You and your divorced partner also need to adhere strictly to the terms of the divorce agreement. For all the emotional turbulence that goes along with adolescence, teenage children generally have a much more objective perspective on the terms of a parental divorce than younger children do. As divorced parents, it will be necessary for both of you to prove to your teenage child that you are each living up to your legal responsibilities.

This is particularly true of a noncustodial parent who must provide court-determined financial assistance (typically in our society, the father). Teenagers have a fine-tuned sense of justice and will be rightfully intolerant of a parent who falls behind in these payments. On a very mundane but significant level, an unanticipated lack of money in the custodial household can have a disastrous effect on a teenager's social life, which is much more expensive than the social life of a younger child and yet very important to a teenager's self-development.

■ *As a single parent, allow your teenager to express whatever feelings come naturally to her or him about both you and your ex-partner.*

A teenager will have different emotional attachments to each parent before, during, and after the divorce. Don't expect her or him to mirror your own feelings toward the absent parent. As adolescent's feelings may go through various changes immediately after the divorce as she or he watches you and the other parent adjust to the new situation.

Even if your teenager feels that the absent parent caused both of you a lot of emotional turmoil, she or he will still miss the absent parent and may wish the absent parent were still living at home. Expect criticism from your teenage child and realize that her or his attachments to you and the other parent are not the same, just as they were not the same before the divorce (a fact that you may or may not have realized).

■ *Keep an open mind about your adolescent's need for a surrogate parent to fill the absent parent's role.*

Teenage boys and girls living with the parent of the opposite gender may need an older role model of their own gender. For example, a boy who lives with his divorced mother may need an older male as a role model if his father cannot—or will not—play a consistent role in his life. The boy may gravitate toward some surrogate figure, such as a teacher, coach, clergyman, or a friend's older brother. Such an attachment can be helpful, particularly in keeping him out of trouble at school or with the law.

If you are the custodial parent, try to honor the child's attachment, giving your approval to the older adult, as long as the relationship stays balanced and healthy. If you are the absent parent, try not to become overly jealous about your teenager's new mentor, realizing that the other adult may be helping to fulfill an important role in your child's life that, because of your absence, you are not able to fulfill completely yourself.

■ *Don't expect each of your teenage children to react the same way to the divorce.*

Young teenagers (approximately thirteen to sixteen) may feel more embarrassed or insecure than older teenagers about being in a single-parent family. In general, young teenagers are more dependent on family activities and identify more closely with the family as a unit. They also get more of a sense of identity from comparisons with their friends, and they may feel different or left out of the general conversation about family life if their friends do not come from divorced families.

Older teenagers are not as sensitive about having divorced parents, often because, by then, they have met a considerable number of other teenagers in similar situations. Compared to younger teenagers, they are much more mature in answering questions about the divorce and feel much less threatened in talking about the absent parent.

Dating and Remarriage

Teenagers can be surprisingly ambivalent about *either* of their divorced parents dating or marrying another person; but their mixed feelings of dread and excitement are especially keen in the case of the *custodial* parent. On the one hand, they are apprehensive about the uncertain nature of the relationship they are going to have with the new person in their parent's life (and, if the parent is marrying someone with kids, with their new stepsiblings). On the other hand, they hope that the loneliness and depression often involved in living in a one-parent household will finally come to an end.

Not all of the teenage child's concerns are so self-centered. Adolescents also harbor a sense of responsibility for their parents' happiness. They may feel guilty if they themselves are dating and having fun while their custodial parent leads a lonely life devoid of romance. A teenage child may view a custodial parent's dating or remarriage as a chance to have this responsibility lifted from her or his shoulders. However, if a particular date or new spouse seems to be causing misery for the custodial parent, the teenager may feel burdened by a new responsibility to become the "rescuer."

Here are some guidelines for assisting your teenager to cope more effectively with your own dating or remarriage:

■ *Be particularly sensitive to your teenager's feelings when you first begin to date after the divorce.*

In the beginning, it is natural and almost inevitable for your teenage child to be jealous of the people you date as a single parent—regardless of whether these people are the same gender as your child. Her or his jealousy in this situation can arise from several causes besides proprietarial competition with the "other man" or "other woman." The most obvious cause is that your dates are in some sense replacing the absent parent to whom the child still feels emotionally loyal, even though the emotions themselves may be conflicted and unresolved.

In addition, your child may resent the time away from home that you are spending on dates. There may even be resentment over the amount of money you spend on dating, buying new clothes, going to movies, or dining out. Some single parents undergo a personality change to please their dates. An observant teenager will pick up on this and may show disapproval.

Your dating life may also be envied by your teenage child to the point of jealousy. Difficult as it may be for you to appreciate, your child may become very upset that you are dating more frequently than she or he does, or attracting more desirable partners, or enjoying more glamorous or expensive dating experiences.

■ *When involving your child in, or informing your child about, dating or marriage plans, be sensitive to your child's need for comfort, security, trust, and choice.*

Wait until you know your new romantic interest fairly well before arranging for her or him and your teenager to spend time together, and allow your teenager to get used to this person gradually. Keep your child informed about your relationship, but don't ask your child to make decisions about it (by saying, for example, "Do you think I should stop seeing Pat [your date]?").

When you make arrangements for your wedding and your married life afterwards, involve your teenager in an appropriately adult manner. Always try to offer choices, rather than imposing decisions, and to appeal to your child's perspective, rather than your own. For example, if you would like your adolescent child to participate in the wedding ceremony, first say so, in general terms; then mention several possible tasks or roles (for example, being a member of the wedding party itself, helping to write invitations, working with you to plan the reception, helping to run errands from time to time, taking care of younger children). When discussing tasks or roles, emphasize that your child might enjoy fulfilling them, instead of that *you* would appreciate having them fulfilled. As much as possible, don't force your child to do something she or he doesn't want to do.

■ *After remarrying, give teenagers a chance to work out their relationships with new family members at their own pace.*

It is natural for teenage children to feel insecure and even fearful when a parent remarries and a new stepparent (and, possibly, new stepsiblings) join the household. How will they be expected to behave? How will their normal patterns of activity be disrupted? What happens if they hate him, her, or it?

During this period of transition, try to let your teenage child find her or his own answers to these questions. You can start by letting your child spend as much time as necessary being with old friends and conducting her or his life as usual, since these relationships and patterns represent sources of positive, life-sustaining stability while your child is struggling to adjust to the new situation at home.

In addition, be especially clear with your new marriage partner about her or his responsibilities in child-rearing, and then explain these responsibilities to your teenage child. It is not necessary to get your child's approval on the arrangements that you've worked out, but it is imperative for your child to understand what is expected and where the lines of authority lie in terms of discipline.

If you and your romantic attachment (and, possibly, his or her children) simply move in together, anticipate the same difficulties to arise as if you were married. Teenagers may be more reluctant, however, to accept an unmarried partner as having disciplinary rights over them, so be sure to spell out clearly in what areas you expect your children to honor your partner as a responsible adult in terms of authority and discipline.

■ *Don't create false illusions about your new marriage partner as a savior.*

Rarely does a new marriage partner enter a family as a savior. Although two parents will probably bring family life back to what seems like a more "normal" scenario, the new parent will probably not be able to solve all the problems between you and your teenager, or bring an end to preexisting sibling rivalry. Be realistic when telling adolescents what they can expect from the marriage. Some of the realistic "plusses" may be a combined income that will help to ease financial difficulties, more opportunities for family activities, or more resources for personal attention and help.

Above all, avoid painting too rosy a picture about what family life will be like, so that your children don't get their hopes too high and then suffer disappointment. Be sure to point out areas where personal adjustments and the curtailing of privileges may be required (such as sharing a bedroom with a sibling or a new stepsibling).

■ *Take accusations of physical, emotional, or sexual abuse by a stepparent or stepsibling seriously, but don't jump to conclusions.*

If your teenage child alludes to abuse by a stepparent or stepsibling, you should let your child know that you take the accusation seriously. In general, it is important for teenagers to feel that their parents believe them and are not ignoring them when they complain about trouble. In a situation involving a new stepparent's or stepsibling's possible abuse, that feeling is greatly intensified. A parent needs to assume, at first, that the accusation is true and to express support for the child. The consequences of doing otherwise are too risky.

Nevertheless, it *is* possible for a teenage child to lie about abuse from a stepparent or stepsibling, usually because the child is jealous of the intruder or suffers from a major personality clash with her or him. Investigate the situation as thoroughly as possible, keeping a close eye on the relationship. If abuse is occurring, take whatever steps are necessary to protect your son or daughter. Start by enlisting the help of a qualified mental-health professional. Also, depending on the nature of the abuse, you may be required by law to report it to legal authorities. (For further guidance, see the section in this book on sexual abuse, p. 20.)

■ *Be mindful that a teenager may see in your new marriage a model for love and romance.*

Adolescents look for models of love and marriage. Your former, failed marriage probably did not present a very positive model, and your teenage child will recognize this. Now with a new partner, you have a chance to correct whatever negative messages about marriage your daughter or son picked up from the first marriage.

A teenager will watch closely to see how you and your partner treat each other and may be exceptionally critical of what you do. Although it is not your job to present the perfect marriage, it is important to realize that your new relationship will make a vital impression on your teenage child's concept of adult love and that your child may be emulating you in her or his own romantic attachments.

■ *Talk to your teenage children about their new stepsiblings, and call upon their growing sense of adulthood to help you weave the younger children into the new family.*

An adolescent *can* be encouraged to take a more active role in making the blended family work. All that's required is some tact, determination, and courage on your part.

Explain that while you have an equal amount of love to give each child, circumstances are going to require that you spend *similar* but not necessarily *equal* amounts of time with each child. For example, a stepdaughter's problems with fourth-grade homework may require you to spend more time with her than you can spend with your teenage child during a certain period of time. This does not mean, however, that you won't also spend some very nice times with your teenage child during this same period.

Also, give clear guidelines to all of your children—stepchildren and biological children—regarding each child's respective possessions, privileges, and rights. Again, these should be age-appropriate, which means they won't always be equal.

Finally, allow your children to conduct and settle their own disputes as much as possible. As an alternative to disputes, encourage positive sibling interactions, especially between your biological children and stepchildren, calling upon your teenager's growing sense of adulthood to set a good example for the younger children.

7.

Substance Abuse

T he United States of America is a drug culture. The majority of its citizens rely on drugs to pursue their normal lives: coffee in the morning to wake up, a cigarette, beer, or glass of wine in the evening to relax, and/or an occasional pill to fight a cold, lose weight, escape depression, or restore bowel regularity.

It's easy for parents to overlook this fact when they consider their teenage child's possible abuse of controlled substances—alcohol being the number-one most-abused substance, followed by amphetamines ("uppers"), barbiturates ("downers"), marijuana, and cocaine. Much of a child's attraction to drugs in general is preconditioned by society at large. In discouraging a child from abusing drugs, parents must accept this reality and be careful to approach the abuse problem with compassion and practical help instead of disbelief, outrage, and condemnation.

By far the most apparent reason why adolescents first begin to experiment with drugs and then go on to become habitual drug abusers is to fit in with their peers. Not only do many adolescents use drugs simply because that's what their friends do (a basic "mirroring" behavior); they also use them in order to feel more comfortable and emotionally in tune with their friends (a more complex "adapting" behavior).

Other apparent reasons why adolescents turn to drug experimentation and abuse are as follows (in no specific order):

■ to cope with loneliness or boredom;

■ to satisfy a personal curiosity—about oneself as well as about individual drugs;

■ to defy rules or authority;

■ to challenge "common sense" (so-called risk-taking behavior);

■ to appear more adult (or not to appear to be a "baby");

■ to transcend a "self" they do not value;

■ to escape specific emotional or psychosomatic pains;

■ to punish themselves (so-called self-destructive behavior);

■ to gain self-confidence or courage.

While it's important to consider and address any of these *apparent* reasons for an individual teenager's drug experimentation and abuse, there is almost always one *underlying* reason why a child incorporates drug use into her or his personal life-style: to experience pleasure. For at least a short time, a drug can help the user feel good or at least better than she or he naturally feels at the time. Unfortunately, if the user becomes addicted to a particular drug (which is very likely, given habitual use of any of the above-mentioned drugs), she or he can't feel good about it.

Here are guidelines for preventing and coping with teenage substance abuse:

■ *Maintain an active involvement in your child's day-to-day life.*

The more you know about what your child does with her or his leisure time, who your child's friends are, and how your child feels, the better able you will be to detect whether your child is using drugs and, if so, to help her or him stop. Encourage your child to share this information with you in a comfortable and trusting manner by arranging to spend time together frequently and regularly.

Assuming your child feels estranged from you or the family as a whole, she or he is all the more susceptible to relying on drugs to feel "at home." To prevent this from happening, always keep the channels of communication open, involve your child in family events, and make sure she or he is aware of your love and interest.

■ *Set a firm and clear policy prohibiting drug use.*

Don't take it for granted that your child knows that using drugs is wrong or that she or he is forbidden to use them. Explicitly state that you do not approve of teenagers using drugs and that you'll do everything you possibly can to keep your child from using them.

At the same time—or times—that you announce this policy, explain the medical, legal, and social reasons for it as well as the consequences your child will face if she or he should violate it. Just be careful to avoid arguing that drug use is forbidden as long as your child remains "under your roof." This type of argument can backfire, encouraging your child to run away, leave home prematurely, or establish a "home base" somewhere else—steps that are likely to escalate the odds that she or he will abuse drugs.

■*Educate your child to handle situations that foster drug use.*
Try role-playing with your child what she or he should say and do if
drugs are being used or offered. Go beyond advising your child simply
to say no, although this response may occasionally work. Develop
together a number of different and more substantive ways to avoid or
refuse drug-use opportunities without losing face with her or his peers.
   Among the possibilities are the following:

REJECTING DRUGS INSTEAD OF THE DRUG OFFERER

■ "I'm saving my brains for something better."

■ "I don't need the poison."

■ "I don't like what it does to me."

■ "I don't like the way it tastes."

■ "That stuff always backfires on me."

OFFERING AN EXCUSE

■ "I'm allergic."

■ "I'm in training for [sport or activity]."

■ "I don't want to mess up the rest of the day."

USING HUMOR

■ "Sorry, not my brand."

■ "I'd rather just watch you guys act stupid."

TAKING THE OFFENSIVE

■ "I can't believe you really use that stuff."

■ "You guys are too smart for that."

■ "Don't ask me that again if you want to stay friends."

OFFERING AN ALTERNATIVE

■ "Let's get some real food instead."

■ "No, I'd rather play [sport or game]."

   Advise your child to walk away if these strategies don't work, either
making an excuse or not, depending on the particular situation. Also,
give your child pointers on how to initiate conversations about rejecting drugs with friends or prospective friends, not only for her or
his personal benefit but also for the friends' benefit.

■ *Educate your child about how to exercise self-control.*
Take every opportunity, whether it involves substance abuse or not, to teach your child the following skills:

- ■ how to set healthy self-development goals;

- ■ how to stick to one's principles;

- ■ how to delay gratification when appropriate;

- ■ how to self-reward and self-discipline based on one's behavior.

The more guidance your child has in such matters, the easier it will be for her or him to resist the most common temptations to use drugs.

If your child is currently wrestling with actual drug-abuse problems, assist in setting up and follow a specific self-improvement program to overcome those problems. Let your child steer this program but hold on to your role as an ongoing consultant.

■ *Motivate your child to participate in activities and assume responsibilities that will make more constructive use of her or his leisure time.*
Given that boredom and low self-esteem are major factors contributing to teenage drug abuse, encourage your child to do things that are personally interesting, challenging, and morale building: sports, physical-fitness programs, volunteer work, hobbies, part-time jobs, home-improvement projects, and/or extension classes.

If possible, guide your child toward activities and responsibilities involving other kids her or his age who are similarly inclined to use their leisure time productively. These kinds of peer experiences can help your child develop social skills and value social interactions that are not oriented around drug use.

■ *As often as practical, arrange for your child to be supervised.*
If it doesn't cause too much trouble, avoid leaving your adolescent child entirely alone when you are away from home for more than a few hours. Get another adult to be there or to look in during your absence. This policy is appropriate for teenagers under any circumstances, but it's especially advisable if you suspect or know that your child has used—or is using—drugs.

In arranging for supervision, try not to imply that you don't trust your child. You don't want your child to feel like a prisoner, and she or he is entitled to a certain amount of independence. However, you also have a responsibility to ensure that both your child and your home are safe and sound. With these objectives in mind, make sure that the supervision is benevolent and discreet.

■ *Seek all available outside help when appropriate.*

To improve your knowledge and understanding of adolescent drug abuse, gather pertinent information from every school, community, and church/synagogue-sponsored drug-prevention program in your area. This information will also help you discuss drug abuse with your child and, if necessary, deal with any abuse problems your child may develop.

Assuming your child already does have an abuse problem, you should also consider enlisting the help of a professional mental-health therapist, psychologist, or psychiatrist. Often a major cause of a drug-abuse problem is a deeply rooted emotional problem. And if your child is already addicted to drugs, she or he will have to go through a considerable amount of emotional turmoil in order to break that addiction.

■ *Punish substance abuse in an appropriate fashion.*

You shouldn't punish your child too severely for casual experimentation with drugs, especially if she or he has confessed to you about it. However, if your child has engaged in relatively heavy drug use, strong, firmly administered punishment is definitely warranted.

Make sure that your child knows in advance what kind of consequences to expect if she or he starts using drugs. This knowledge may help act as a deterrent.

Ideally, such consequences should include measures that work directly toward keeping your child away from drugs: for example, prohibiting your child from participating in certain events, friendships, or activities that can be associated with her or his drug use. It might also include general "grounding" and/or a reduction or withdrawal of privileges.

By all means avoid referring to *rehabilitative* steps, like attending drug counseling programs or spending more time doing homework, as "punishments." Instead, they should be presented to your child as helpful, rewarding, and unique opportunities to turn her or his life around.

■ *Set a good example.*

It's difficult to convince a teenager not to indulge in controlled substances if the teenager sees her or his parents doing so. Restrict any such indulgence on your part as much as possible, try not to indulge in the presence of your child, and avoid referring to your own drug taking, or another adult's, in favorable terms (e.g., "I need a drink to relax" or "He's much nicer when he's had a few drinks").

In addition, explain to your child the developmental, social, and legal reasons why you and other adults *can* indulge to a certain extent in controlled substances while she or he and other teenagers *cannot*. Make sure that your child understands and accepts these distinctions.

Your child should also know that you have personal rules regulating your drug use: strict limits regarding kinds of drugs, amounts, rate of intake, occasions when you'll allow yourself to take drugs, and what you will and won't do while under the influence of drugs (such as not driving). State these rules specifically so that your child can use them later as possible models governing her or his drug consumption in adulthood.

Signs of Possible Substance Abuse

■ any dramatic change for the worse in behavior, appearance, school performance, friends, or sleeping/eating patterns

■ frequent incidents of memory lapse, sluggishness, or incoherent speech (e.g., unfinished sentences, irrational statements)

■ non-illness-related pupil dilation, bloodshot eyes, runny nose, cough, vomiting

■ repeated incidents of clumsiness or loss of coordination

■ major swings in mood (e.g., from depressed to elated) or energy level (e.g., from lethargic to hyperactive)

■ frequent inappropriate responses to outside events (e.g., unprovoked anger, insensitive laughter, unwarranted fear)

■ repeated incidents of lying, stealing, or criminal behavior

■ frequent failure to appear as promised, be on time, or meet responsibilities

■ increasing secretiveness, preoccupation, withdrawal, and avoidance

■ general loss of motivation and former interests

■ escalated use of breath and air fresheners (or such odor maskers as heavy perfumes and incense)

■ possession of drug-related paraphernalia (e.g., flasks, cigarette papers, rollers, plastic Baggies, pipes, scales, pill bottles, coke spoons, razor blades, needles, atomizer bottles, butane minitorches)

■ possession of items referring to drug use (e.g., books, magazines, recordings, printed T-shirts, posters, videocassettes, artwork)

■ frequent reference to drugs in word choices, jokes, and conversations

■ chronic and otherwise inexplicable lack or abundance of money

The Dangers of Substance Abuse

ALCOHOL

■ has a much greater impact on teenagers than adults due to smaller body size of teenagers;

■ is a natural depressant that ultimately results in listlessness, apathy, and despair;

■ impairs coordination and slows reflexes;

■ increases one's vulnerability to physical and mental coercion;

■ causes indigestion, nausea, headache, and such "hangover" symptoms as hypersensitivity and shakiness;

■ reduces inhibitions so that emotional impressions and displays are out of one's control;

■ can cause unpredictable memory "blackouts";

■ over time, weakens the immune system, ruins the complexion, damages the liver and brain, and induces psychoses.

BARBITURATES ("DOWNERS")

■ can trigger unpredictable stupor, loss of consciousness, and even death;

■ are highly addictive, necessitating increasing amounts for equal effect;

■ can result in sleepiness, confusion, despair, uncontrollable crying "jags," and loss of coordination;

■ increase, over time, general irritability and impatience;

■ can render one exceptionally vulnerable to physical and mental coercion;

■ can cause headache and "hangover" symptoms.

AMPHETAMINES ("UPPERS")

■ increase restlessness and irritability;

■ can induce feelings of anger and paranoia;

■ result in loss of coordination and muscle control;

■ produce, over time, insomnia, skin disorders, damage to the digestive system, and/or convulsions;

■ are highly addictive, necessitating increasing amounts for equal effect;

■ can trigger hallucinations;

■ render one incapable of completing thoughts or concentrating on tasks;

■ can have emotionally and physically exhausting "crash" aftereffects.

MARIJUANA

■ diminishes short-term memory, with permanent damage over time;

■ results in dramatic loss of initiative and, ultimately, energy;

■ can occasionally induce paranoia and hallucinations;

■ causes severe misjudgments regarding time and space;

■ can disrupt, over time, menstrual cycle and reduce sperm count;

■ damages the lungs (as much as one pack of cigarettes per joint);

■ is attended by long-lasting aftereffects, including difficulty in concentrating and problems in coordinating thoughts and movements.

COCAINE

■ causes general irritability and anxiety;

■ can trigger unpredictable psychosis, heart failure, respiratory collapse, and death;

■ dramatically impairs physical reflexes and judgment;

■ results, over time, in depression and loss of initiative;

■ is highly addictive, necessitating increasing amounts for equal effect.

Resources

American Council for Drug Education
5820 Hubbard Drive
Rockville, MD 20852
(301) 984-5700

National Federation of Parents for Drug-Free Youth
1820 Farnwell Avenue, Suite 16
Silver Spring, MD 20902
(800) 544-5437

Parent Resource Institute on Drug Education
100 Edgewood Avenue, Suite 1216
Atlanta, GA 30303
(800) 241-9746

Alcoholics Anonymous
Box 459, Grand Central Station
New York, NY 10163
(check local telephone directory for local chapter)

Al-Anon and Alateen
(for relatives and friends of alcohol abusers)
P.O. Box 862, Midtown Station
New York, NY 10018
(check local telephone directory for local chapter)

Alcohol and Drug Helpline
(800) 252-6465

Cocaine Hotline
(800) COCAINE (262-2463)

8.

Running Away

Hanging over the teenage years for every child, especially the car-driving years after age sixteen, is the question "What will life be like when I leave home?" One in seven children between the ages of thirteen and sixteen and one in five children between the ages of sixteen and eighteen actually run away from home to find out.

For some of these children, running away from home is primarily a sincere, if misguided, effort to achieve independence. For others, it's primarily a gesture of defiance aimed at parents who are viewed as uncaring, overly strict, or otherwise intolerable. For both groups, it's a sign of emotional instability.

Instead of arranging to leave home in a mature and responsible fashion or attempting to resolve their problems while staying at home, runaways are simply trying to escape pain. In doing so, they are taking a rash flight away from the known but apparently unacceptable into the unknown and definitely unpredictable.

Since the outside world is so dangerous, teenagers who are upset emotionally and cut off from home can easily get into trouble. Trying to survive on their own, they might wind up sick, broke, hungry, and without shelter; they might be robbed, beaten, sexually abused, or seduced into a life of drugs or crime; or they might even resort to victimizing others, in which case they invite anger and retaliation.

Just as dangerous and unpredictable, however, is the *internal* world of the teenage runaway: that is, the child's *emotional* state once she or he has abandoned the relative security of the home. A teenage runaway can quickly be overwhelmed by feelings of fear, guilt, remorse, shame, foolishness, worthlessness, self-hatred, and depression.

These negative feelings can penetrate deeply and last for a long time, darkly coloring the runaway's sense of self and the world at large. This happens even in cases when the running-away experience is fairly brief and uneventful, followed by a return to home life as usual. Assuming the running-away experience is especially negative or the reentry into home life is poorly managed, then the chance that the runaway will suffer seriously from such negative feelings is quite high.

Most teenagers who run away ultimately come back home on their own, usually within one to three days and usually in a contrite frame of mind. Most of them will try running away again, usually several times in the course of their teenage years.

Indeed, while *any* history of repeated attempts to run away needs to be taken very seriously, most are not causes for unusual alarm unless they include more than one runaway attempt during a given three-month period, coupled with little or no initiative on the part of the returning runaway to try to make her or his home life succeed. In these latter cases, psychiatric intervention is almost always warranted, given the strong indication that the runaway child and her or his family are unable to work out matters for themselves, even on a short-term basis.

Here are some guidelines to help you work out matters successfully with your runaway, or would-be runaway, teenage child:

■ *Watch for signs that your child may be considering running away.*

Teenagers don't often announce beforehand their intentions to run away. Instead, their parents have to be on the lookout for clues. This is especially true in the following situations:

> ■ The teenager wants to run away because she or he feels neglected by her or his parents. Feeling this way, the teenager plans secretly in order to fulfill the self-torturing fantasy: "My parents won't even notice I've gone." She or he assumes that once they *do* notice, they will be all the more guilt stricken.

> ■ The teenager wants to go it alone but simply can't face hurting her or his parents in person. In this kind of situation, the teenager actually believes she or he is acting out of love and is left with no other reasonable choice but to depart in this manner.

> ■ The teenager wants to run away out of a feeling of guilt, shame, or embarrassment. Typically, such teenagers believe that they have irretrievably failed their parents' expectations or that they are a burden to their parents or would become so if they stayed.

With these possible situations in mind, be extra alert for running-away clues during particularly stressful times for your child (e.g., a romantic crisis), for you and your child (e.g., an ongoing argument), or for your family as a whole (e.g., a divorce, a household move, or an economic crisis). Be especially loving and supportive toward your child during such times so that she or he will be less likely to contemplate running away.

Here are the most common "unspoken" running-away clues:

■ a recent marked and steady increase in the time your child spends away from home, especially if such absences tend to be unexplained;

■ a sustained and otherwise inexplicable effort on your child's part to accumulate money and/or resources;

■ an increase in the number of "secret" phone conversations, correspondence, and meetings;

■ an unusual and otherwise inexplicable "cleaning up" of possessions and affairs (perhaps including giving things away);

■ an unusual and otherwise inexplicable effort to clear away a block of time in the near future or to avoid—or cancel—plans for the near future.

If any of these clues, or others, give you reason to suspect that your child may be considering running away, try talking with her or him honestly and comfortably about your concerns and about what is going on in her or his life. Remember that there may in fact be no connection between the two.

You don't necessarily have to confront your child directly with your suspicions that she or he may be planning to run away. But you should make every effort to dispel some of the mysteries that are cropping up between you and your child and to improve your person-to-person relationship.

■ *Avoid directly or indirectly daring your child to leave home.* Try as much as possible not to use phrases like "As long as you're living under this roof . . ." or "Not in my house, you aren't" or "Once you get out on your own, you're free to do what you want." Such statements encourage your child to imagine a better world outside the home. In certain particularly stressful situations, she or he may even follow such implicit suggestions to run away simply in order to make you regret what you've said and, by extension, your style as a parent in general.

Never allow yourself to get so carried away with anger or exasperation that you say something like "I can't wait until you get out on your own" or "Go ahead, leave home, see if I care." Don't say such things even in a spirit of mocking humor. They can resonate in your insecure teenage child's psyche much more profoundly than you can imagine.

■ *Respond calmly but firmly to any direct threat to run away that your child makes.*

If your teenage child does express an inclination or an intention to run away, take it very seriously. It may well be that your child doesn't actually mean what she or he says. In many cases, an expression of this nature is no more than a masked cry for more attention, affection, or respect. Nevertheless, you can't afford to assume that your child won't carry out her or his threat, if only to save face.

Whenever your child makes such a threat, tell her or him immediately, and in no uncertain terms, that you love her or him and that you don't want her or him to run away. Then try to use the occasion to talk more honestly and openly about the things that are bothering her or him. Perhaps these conversations will help both of you work out some mutually acceptable changes at home that will preclude any future thoughts on your child's part about running away. In any event, the most important thing for you to do during these conversations is to *listen* to your child so that she or he feels heard. Many times, this kind of attention is all that's required to remedy matters.

■ *Don't cooperate in your child's running away.*

Assuming your child is determined to leave home, don't make it easy for her or him to do so. Rather than passively allowing your child to go away, restate your disapproval of this strategy and do what you reasonably can to stop her or him from acting upon it.

You might try to engage your child in exploring alternatives to running away, depending on the situation at hand and on the resources that are available. Maybe your child could spend a brief period away from home with a relative or a friend whom both of you trust and respect. Maybe you could both seek professional counseling to improve your relationship. Maybe your child would be satisfied to spend some time away from home in the near future, either with you (e.g., on a special outing or vacation) or by her- or himself (e.g., at a camp or job site).

You might also want to let your would-be runaway child know what the consequences will be if she or he should actually run away. Be sure she or he realizes, for example, the goods, resources, and services that will be forsaken; the problems likely to be encountered in trying to live away from home; and, if relevant, the stricter rules that will have to be imposed (especially regarding time allowed away from home and reporting procedures) upon her or his return.

This latter kind of conversation has to be handled carefully. You don't want it to degenerate into an angry tirade, you don't want to make exaggerated statements that will inspire disbelief and contempt on your child's part, and above all, you don't want to imply to your child that there's no turning back once she or he has left. On the other hand, you *do* want your child to have a realistic picture of what to expect. Children caught up in the drama of running away are apt to have a very distorted sense of things.

Express yourself calmly, with due consideration for your child's seriousness and self-esteem. First, ask for your child's patience in hearing you out. Then state your case. Finally, request that your child take some time to think about what you have said before doing anything that she or he might regret and that you most definitely can't condone. This thinking period, which honors—and appeals to—your child's sense of reason, will provide your child with an opportunity to decide *not* to run away without losing face.

■ *If your child does run away, make every reasonable effort to locate her or him as soon as possible and to encourage her or him to return.*

Too many dangerous possibilities await the teenage runaway for her or his parents to assume a wait-and-see role, hoping that their child will come to her or his senses sooner rather than later. Remember that most runaway teenagers want—in fact, need—their parents to pay more attention to them, which would certainly include looking for them if they should run away and then trying to get them to come back home.

Immediately upon suspecting or discovering that your child has run away, try contacting anyone and everyone who may know her or his whereabouts. Personally investigate places where she or he may have gone. And notify the police right away. They may not be authorized to conduct an official search until a certain period of time has gone by (usually twenty-four hours), but they can provide you with possible leads and strategies for your own search efforts based on their experience with numerous different types of situations involving teenage runaways.

■ *Throughout the time your child is involved in running away, distinguish between the pain you are feeling or causing yourself and that which your child is feeling or causing.*

When their teenage child runs away, most parents are understandably consumed with worry, which leaves them vulnerable to all sorts of other negative and energy-draining emotions. By far the most common feeling is that they have lost control of their child. Parents of runaways need to work hard to disabuse themselves of the feeling that they *should* be able to control their child.

A teenage child has a mind of her or his own and is capable of acting on her or his own. While it may be appropriate for parents to regret specific things that they did or did not do in the course of raising their child, it is not appropriate for parents to blame themselves for *not* controlling their teenage child. Nor should they blame their child for wanting to be independent.

If your child has run away, stay focused on those emotions that are not self-punishing or punitive toward your child. Although you may not be able to help feeling rejected, try to bear in mind that runaway teenagers are almost always motivated, consciously or subconsciously, by a desire to get their parents to care more for them or to care for them in a different, more agreeable manner. In other words, they are not motivated by a desire to be rid of their parents' care. In effect, they're running away to try to make *you* feel the pain of separation and miscommunication that *they* feel.

Given this aspect of most teenage runaway situations, your most appropriate and constructive emotional response—that is, the emotional frame of mind you should try hardest to maintain—is compassion and love for your child and acceptance and forgiveness of yourself. Recognizing these truths will help you cope more easily with your child's running away and ultimately restore the relationship with your child.

■ *Welcome your child back with love, compassion, and concern.* When your child returns home, either voluntarily or under your guidance, your first and foremost act should be to express your love for her or him and your joy that she or he is back. Many ex–runaway children can't help but display excitement about being back home; but whether or not they do, they're bound to be very emotionally confused at that time, feeling awkward and embarrassed at best and devastated and ashamed at worst. Your warm reception will do wonders to restore your child's sense of self-worth and to set both of you on the path to a better relationship.

You may feel compelled to introduce new policies aimed at closer supervision of your child, especially if you cited them before she or he ran away as possible consequences of a running-away attempt. However, avoid punishing your child for the attempt to run away. It can't do any good, and it can do a considerable amount of harm, instantly and automatically reviving the worst images she or he may have of your authoritarianism and lack of understanding.

■ *After your runaway child returns, be prepared to make changes in your home life and in your relationship with your child.*

As soon as your child has had sufficient time to settle down and feel somewhat natural at home—say, after two or three days—you and your child should arrange to spend some private, uninterrupted time together discussing how the home-life situation might be improved so that your child won't feel driven to run away and you won't feel obligated to behave like her or his jailer.

First, set up a specific time for this meeting with your child and let her or him know the purpose of it: to work out a more satisfying home life. That way, both of you can prepare for the meeting in advance. Then, having thought before the meeting of various possibilities concerning the future, establish in your own mind what you might reasonably expect your child to do, what you yourself might be willing to do, and where you feel you might have to draw certain lines. Finally, use the meeting itself to come to mutually acceptable terms with your child on how things will be in the future so that after the meeting both of you can get on with your lives—separately as well as together.

9.
Overeating

The leading nutritional problem among American children is obesity. A quarter of the population between ages thirteen and twenty suffers from it, with male and female sufferers in roughly equal proportions. According to the U.S. Public Health Service, a teenager is technically considered obese if she or he is 20 percent over her or his ideal weight; and by far the most common reason why a teenager becomes and remains obese is overeating.

Although overeating may be the main *physical* cause of obesity, there are almost always significant *emotional* causes. An obese child typically overeats to compensate for being undernourished emotionally. Perhaps she or he feels neglected, incompetent, or inferior in some way. Maybe she or he is experiencing trouble dealing with day-to-day stress in her or his home life, school life, or social life. Possibly she or he is bothered—consciously or subconsciously—by a specific psychological conflict, such as a phobia about becoming ill or a suppressed desire to inflict harm on someone.

Whatever the case, overeaters in general tend to have low self-esteem, which, in turn, leads to poor self-control and difficulty in making decisions. Unfortunately, low self-esteem is not only the most common emotional *cause* but also the most common emotional *effect* of overeating. Thus, teenage overeaters find themselves caught in a vicious circle: They don't care about themselves, which gives them an excuse to indulge in eating behavior that is not good for them, which makes them disgusted with themselves, which leads them not to care about themselves, and so on.

The long-range consequences of overeating can be devastating. Emotionally, an overeater may fall victim to chronic depression or anxiety. Physically, she or he may develop heart disease, high blood pressure, a high cholesterol level, difficulty in breathing, or a blood-sugar irregularity. Any one of these conditions, emotional or physical, can reduce life expectancy.

Unfortunately, the most obvious solution to overeating, dieting, is not necessarily the best solution. In many instances, the stresses and strains of trying to maintain a diet only aggravate the overeater's problems with self-esteem, self-control, and self-satisfaction. Every time an overeater fails to stick to her or his diet, she or he can become even more hopeless and self-punishing about the obesity, which increases the chances of discontinuing dieting altogether and resuming overeating on a regular basis.

Such diet-related problems are common to people of any age, but they are compounded in the teenager living at home. Even if the dieter's parents try to stay as far removed from their child's efforts as possible, they are still close enough to witness all the inevitable struggles, frustrations, and setbacks associated with them.

Most of the time, the teenage dieter's parents are *not* far removed from their child's diet. Instead, they feel personally obliged, or are directly recruited, to become active partners in their child's diet, helping their child plan it, motivating her or him to stick with it, and organizing meals to accommodate it.

In either case, but especially in the latter, the parent-child relationship can easily and quickly become soured by mutual resentment, disappointment, and exasperation. The same thing can happen when an obese teenager initiates, or is coerced into following, a strict exercise program to lose weight. Anytime the teenager fails to meet the demands of such a program, she or he may also feel like a failure in the eyes of her or his parents, regardless of how sensitive or detached those parents try to be.

Avoiding such problems does not mean abandoning all efforts aimed at influencing your obese child to eat more responsibly and exercise more extensively. It's simply a matter of degree. The gradual introduction of a mild, informal trend toward eating healthier foods in more modest portions at less frequent intervals stands a much better chance of creating a positive and lasting change in your child's eating habits than the sudden imposition of a drastic and detailed diet. A gradual, mild, and informal approach also works better to get your child more productively involved in exercise.

If your child is obese or a chronic overeater, consider taking the following steps:

■ *Check for every possible physical cause of your child's obesity.* Before doing anything else, you and your child should consult a physician. Find out if there is any constitutional factor contributing to your child's obesity or overeating: for example, sluggish thyroid activity, a blood-sugar problem, anemia, or a food allergy. Although these conditions are relatively rare among obese teenagers, it's best to test for them as soon as possible.

Also, ask the physician for dietary and exercise recommendations.

While you may not want detailed plans (for reasons already stated), you can definitely profit from expert general advice.

■ *Inform your child about good eating and exercise habits without nagging.*

Guard against assuming the role of a coach. Instead, assume the less active and therefore less abrasive role of an adviser. In other words, be prepared to help your child as much as she or he wants without taking it upon yourself to force your child to help her- or himself.

To be a good adviser, first become informed about common-sense foods, eating habits, and exercise routines that are healthy and practical for teenagers in general and have a good chance of appealing to your child in particular. Then use this information not only to educate your overweight child whenever an opportunity presents itself but also to guide your "normal" planning of family meals and recreation.

Be careful not to initiate talk about healthy eating or healthy exercise too often or to lecture at length when you talk. Share your knowledge with your child at appropriate times in your ongoing dialogue—that is, when you and your child are already talking about such matters, when your child actually asks you about them, or when it's obvious that your child is doing something inappropriate due to a lack of information about diet or nutrition.

To test whether you may be overdoing your role as an adviser, keep track of each time you talk with your child about food, exercise, or being overweight, both when the discussion occurred and what specifically you said. If these occasions tend to occur more than once or twice a week or if, as a whole, they represent a sizable percentage of the total number of times that the two of you have a serious conversation, then you are probably pressuring your child too much. Saying the same things about your child's weight problem over and over again clearly does not help the situation.

In addition, avoid at all times making statements that will cause your child to feel unduly guilty or embarrassed about being overweight, such as, "You'd be so much prettier if you'd only lose ten pounds!" or "How can you just stuff yourself like that?" or "Don't be such a pig." Instead, emphasize the overall health value that every human being derives from maintaining an appropriate weight and always express confidence in your child's ability to achieve this goal for him- or herself.

■ *Establish and enforce sensible policies regarding family meals and mealtimes.*

Among the policies to consider adopting in your household are the following:

■ Have rules about regular mealtimes and snack times. Stick to the rules so that your child does not wind up eating or snacking whenever it's personally convenient or desirable.

■ Set appropriate limits on the total amount of food you make available at mealtimes. Then let each person fill her or his own plate. This makes your child personally responsible for monitoring her or his food intake, and it prevents you from inadvertently giving your child more food than she or he wants or needs.

■ Be sensible in your food shopping and menu planning. Cut out exceedingly rich foods but don't eliminate all sauces or desserts. Introduce more fruits and vegetables into your family's diet gradually rather than abruptly. Minor adjustments are much easier to accept and much more likely to last than major ones.

■ Shop, plan menus, and cook according to a regular schedule. The more control you build in to food purchasing and preparation, the less chance there is for "trouble" foods or meals to wind up on your table. Make all members of the family aware of these routines so that they will all develop more respect for food purchasing and preparation.

■ *Make sure that all meals take place in a relaxed and pleasant environment.*

Encouraging your child to look forward to eating experiences rather than to eating in itself will change her or his entire attitude toward food. The more aesthetically and socially appealing mealtimes are, the less inclined your child will be either to derive pleasure simply from shoveling food into her or his mouth or to eat food thoughtlessly, without appreciating what—or how much—is being consumed.

As much as possible, transform each mealtime into a special occasion on which to enjoy not only the food but also pleasant physical surroundings and easygoing, nonbusiness-oriented conversation. The serving area should be attractive and compelling, and so should the food presentation itself. Also, eliminate distractions; for example, don't eat in front of the television set and don't answer the telephone during meals.

■ *Involve your child in choosing and preparing healthy foods.*

Your child already thinks about food a great deal, so why not capitalize on this interest? She or he will be much more motivated to eat judiciously upon assuming an active role in putting healthy food on the table.

Take your child grocery shopping with you and look together for nourishing as well as taste-tempting foods that are low in fat and calories. Plan, tend, and harvest a garden together, whether it's an indoor herb garden in front of a sunny window or a full-fledged vegetable garden in the backyard. Finally, work together to turn the foods you have purchased and grown into sensible as well as delicious meals.

■ Don't use food as a punishment or reward.
Resist the temptation to celebrate your obese child's achievements and good fortune with snacks, favorite dishes, or fancy desserts. Conversely, don't forbid or withhold such food items to indicate your displeasure with your child. Otherwise, you'll be inadvertently training your child to associate eating with happiness and not eating with unhappiness.

In addition, try to avoid directly linking food with love, for example, by saying, "I baked this cake especially for you" or "I know how much you like macaroni and cheese." Moreover, do not use food as a pacifier, for example, by serving popcorn or potato chips to your child in the evening as a means of soothing restlessness. As much as possible, you should be influencing your obese child to regard eating as a pleasant life-supporting activity rather than as a form of recreation, relaxation, or emotional self-management.

■ Seek opportunities to praise your child and acknowledge her or his strong points.
A significantly overweight child is one who is not happy with her- or himself. If you can raise this child's self-esteem, you'll also be increasing her or his interest in making positive and lasting changes in eating and exercise habits.

Be alert for occasions when you can express sincere admiration for your child's behavior and accomplishments. Encourage your child to engage in activities that are likely to bolster her or his pride, self-confidence, and sense of accomplishment.

■ Examine your child's home life, school life, and social life for stress factors.
Regularly talk with your child about what's going on in her or his world and keep your ears open for any signs of experiencing an emotionally distressing problem. Alleviating this problem may release your child from an inner compulsion to overeat.

Also, do whatever you reasonably can to create and maintain a happy and stress-free environment at home, especially during times when your child regularly eats (snack times as well as mealtimes). Make sure that your child gets frequent, regular, and dependable personal attention of a nonjudgmental nature and that others in the family treat her or him with respect.

■*Consider arranging for a professional evaluation of your child's emotional well-being.*

If you suspect that there are specific emotional issues troubling your child—especially if she or he manifests emotional disturbance in ways other than overeating—don't hesitate to consult a psychiatrist, psychologist, or other mental-health professional. Begin by asking for a general evaluation. Then, if the evaluation warrants it, you can arrange for this person to treat your child.

In any event, bear in mind that it is much easier to conquer an overeating problem during the teenage years than during the adult years, and the odds of an overeating teenager turning into an overeating adult are very high. If your obese teenager is having no success conquering her or his overeating problems after several years despite her or his best efforts coupled with your best efforts, then it may be advisable to seek professional help whether or not you suspect an underlying emotional problem.

At PCGC:
Helping Obese Teenagers

One of the most daunting tasks any individual can face is achieving and maintaining an ideal weight; but for adolescents, who are going through uniquely dramatic physical and life-style changes, this task can be especially difficult. The challenge for psychotherapists is to devise treatment modes that affect multiple, complex aspects of an obese teenager's life, not just a diet-and-exercise regimen, in order to encourage weight loss and stabilization.

One of the pioneering responses to this challenge has been PCGC's Adolescent Weight Management Study. It focuses on the adolescent subgroup that most commonly needs help in weight management: girls between ages fourteen and sixteen who have to lose forty or more pounds in order to reach their ideal weight. Although the study itself features a program of *professional* intervention in specific cases of obesity, its primary aim is to assist *families* in managing such cases. The guiding philosophy of the study is that the family is often at the root of a teenager's obesity problem.

To date, the study has confirmed the following specific ways in which the family most commonly contributes to an obese teenager's overeating:

■ by insisting—or implying—that everybody's plate must be cleaned, a typical phenomenon in households governed by parents who were raised under restrictive economic circumstances;

■ by equating food with love, that is, by functioning as if dispensing huge amounts of food were the same as doling out similar amounts of love and, conversely, as if eating large servings of food were the same as receiving a great deal of love;

■ by using food for the express purpose of pacifying emotional pain—a psychosomatic "nursing" approach that sometimes works but never more than temporarily;

■ by depending too much on food—or occasions when food is served—to unite family members, an especially prevalent tactic within families that are experiencing interpersonal conflicts.

The experiences encountered in the PCGC Adolescent Weight Management Study also suggest that heredity and environment are equally responsible for causing obesity in teenage children. Most overweight children do come from overweight families. And in some of these cases biological factors are being passed along from parent to child that make the body store more fat than usual, as if to protect the individual against famine. But just as frequently, biological factors are *not* contributing to a family's tendency toward obesity. Instead, family members as a rule—often from generation to generation—are inclined to fall victim to *situational* factors that promote obesity: a high-fat, high-calorie diet and/or the type of bad eating habits and attitudes mentioned above.

Among the recommendations for at-home weight management that have emerged from the study so far are the following:

■ Address obesity problems seriously as soon as they appear in a child's life. It's much easier to tackle and reverse obesity at an earlier age than at a later one.

■ Remember that there's a strong link between depression and obesity; that is, either condition can easily lead to, and sustain, the other condition. With this in mind, parents of an obese child should be on the alert for possible overeating problems if their child appears depressed and for possible depression problems if their child is obese or appears to be overeating.

■ In order for a child to lose weight, it's absolutely critical that she or he believes in her or his ability to do so. Therefore, parents of obese children should always express confidence in their child's efforts to lose weight and maintain weight loss. They should also assist their child in following sensible weight-losing strategies that offer the greatest chance for step-by-step success.

10.
Planning for the Future

Adolescence is a time to begin planning for the future, for the time when your teenage child will leave home and start out on her or his own. Individual teenagers may not *show* much concern for the future, but that doesn't mean that it isn't there, influencing their moods and motivating their behavior. All teenagers feel emotionally pressured by the need to make vocational and career decisions during their high school years, and they are continually weighing the options that lie before them, sometimes on a conscious level but much more often on a subconscious level.

Conscious, active planning for the future is generally an on-again, off-again enterprise, even for the most conscientious teenager. It can encompass both the most unlikely career fantasies—for example, a shy, gawky child "planning" to be a movie star or a restless, nonacademic child "planning" to be an archeologist—as well as some very appropriate, realistic, and insightful choices. Parents should not expect or require their adolescent children to be consistent in their dreams and decisions about what they want to do with their lives. Otherwise, they may discourage their children from engaging in the planning process at all.

One of the major sources of stress and estrangement between teenagers and their parents is arguing about future plans or the lack thereof. Therefore, you need to proceed gently, with a great deal of faith, hope, and forbearance. Encourage your child to develop plans. Listen supportively when she or he shares plans with you, and tactfully guide your child to make choices that are realistic, well-informed, and likely to engage her or his talents and enthusiasm.

For the most part, beginning high school students already recognize and accept the fact that they will soon have to leave home and shoulder responsibilities that were formerly their parents'. They also feel that they must start demonstrating, both to their parents and themselves, that they can live independently of the family and home environment. The actual "break" from home is seldom sudden and complete at a given age. Instead, the transition to adulthood and independence is gradual and may require several years after high school or even college.

Your role as a parent is a tricky one. Just as your child needs to break away from home emotionally, you need to break away from the parent-child relationship that you had in the past. You must relinquish more and more of your authority while you allow your child the freedom to assume more and more control over her or his own life. At the same time, you must always "hang around" in case your help is requested. This means remaining sensitive to your child's changing needs without necessarily intervening, accepting mistakes as much as you can, and being open-minded and flexible when she or he calls upon you for assistance.

To help your child plan for an emotionally satisfying and fulfilling future as an independent adult, here are some important guidelines:

■ *See that you and your child meet regularly with the school guidance counselor.*

Soon after your teenager begins high school, if not before, you should meet together with one of the school's guidance counselors to discuss the program of courses the school offers in terms of various career options. In this discussion, as well as in future ones, let your child take the lead in asking questions and giving responses. You can prepare in advance by helping your child draw up a list of questions, concerns, or issues. This strategy will help ensure that you don't cause resentment in your child by trying to run her or his affairs.

A guidance counselor can give your child *and* you valuable information that can save both of you a considerable amount of confusion, regret, and anguish later on. Often the minimum requirements to graduate are not specifically focused for college entry or professional training. Although your child probably does not know for sure what she or he wants to do at this early stage, it is important to know what the options are and what courses or programs will be necessary when she or he does select a major for a specific post–high school career.

A counselor can also advise you and your teenager on the different colleges that she or he might be interested in—and qualify for—and help you evaluate them in terms of academic programs, costs, and career training. It is not too early, even in the first year of high school, to begin taking courses that will fulfill entrance requirements for college. Encourage your child to accept advanced placement courses or enrollment in an honors program if she or he qualifies, because this kind of background is always viewed very highly by college recruiters.

■ *Guide your teenager toward taking high school seriously even if she or he does not plan to go to college.*

Sometimes adolescents choose not to go to college, whether or not they can afford it, often because it holds little interest for them in terms of what they plan to do for a living. Nevertheless, this is not a valid reason for a child to drift through high school, without concern for courses, grades, or extracurricular activities.

First of all, don't let your children simply dismiss college-related courses as irrelevant. Many young people do not appreciate the need for at least some college-related training until after they've been working for a few years. You don't want to nag your teenage child about taking college preparatory courses. However, you should seize appropriate opportunities to discuss with your child the value of taking some college-related courses during high school in order to prevent having to take them later on, when it is much more burdensome to do so.

Even if your child never does go on to college, a well-balanced and challenging high school curriculum is important. This may be the last time she or he is exposed to the arts, humanities, and sciences. Regardless of career choice, your child will have to succeed in a literate and information-driven society. A broad academic background is a handy passport to many social and cultural opportunities.

■ *Be aware that your influence over your child's plans for the future is limited.*

Parents exert a substantial but limited influence over their teenage children's career choices. As a role model, your impact on a child's choice of career depends to a great extent on your relationship with her or him. Teenagers who are not on good terms with their parents may reject their parents' life-style and career decisions out of sheer rebelliousness or as part of a more concerted effort to prove their independence. On the other hand, adolescents who admire their parents and get along well may be drawn to the same careers and life goals as their parents. Certainly, in the latter case, teenage children will take parental advice and suggestions more seriously.

Nevertheless, you cannot and should not make life decisions for your adolescents. Most likely they will make their own choices, even in the face of your objections. It is best to let them make their own mistakes and learn from them, always certain that you will be there to help them recover and start over.

You cannot live your children's lives for them. You cannot force them to avoid mistakes they will undoubtedly make as they test their maturity and independence. It is better to let them fail and then help them get over the failure than to stand in their way and run the risk that they will later resent you for not having trusted them.

■ *Try to appreciate the intense pressures on your child to make a vocational choice while in high school.*

Often by age twelve a child will begin thinking maturely about what she or he wants to do later in life. By the senior year of high school, the pressure to make a wise and winning choice becomes extremely intense. As a parent, you need to be especially careful to exert just the right amount of influence yourself—not too little, and definitely not too much. On the one hand, children tire of constantly being asked by parents, relatives, peers, and teachers what they want to do when they grow up. Often they feel the need to commit themselves to an answer even though they don't have sufficient information or personal experience to evaluate either the choice itself or their ability to succeed and be happy with it.

Keep in mind that your child will go through different stages of commitment. Up to around age twelve, she or he will have *fantasies* about possible career choices. They are not necessarily realistic, firm, or long lasting. During high school, children make more concrete decisions, but these are usually *tentative* and may change as the child gains knowledge and experience. By senior year or age eighteen, your child should demonstrate more *realistic* thinking about careers or vocations based on interest, talent, and opportunity. As a parent, try to evaluate the type of thinking your child is engaged in—fantasy, tentative, or realistic—and respond and support her or him accordingly.

■ *Keep the lines of communication open when your teenager leaves home.*

It is natural to worry about your teenage child when she or he finally leaves home. A major cause of worry is not knowing what is going on in her or his life. You must keep this worry in proportion and not let it make you feel that you and your child are no longer bound together. When adolescent children live in a college dormitory or in a rented apartment, they may be separated from their parents *physically,* but most children can't—and don't want to—separate themselves from their parents *emotionally* to anywhere near the same degree.

Bearing this ongoing connection in mind, you have an undeniable need to know how things are going for your children after they leave home, but you must walk a fine line between snooping into their private lives and being ready to help out when they are really in trouble. Make it clear that you want to be informed about their lives, but leave it up to them to determine how much they will tell you. Keeping the lines of communication open on your end will reassure your daughter or son that you will be there when she or he needs you.

■ *Be prepared for desperate calls for money.*

Money-related quarrels can play havoc with the emotions of both parent and child as they each go their separate ways during the first year of the child's independence from home. It is best simply to expect—and plan for—periodic emergency calls from your child for money. To keep these calls to a minimum, work out in advance an agreed-upon system for providing funds: either a lump sum at the beginning or monthly deposits into the child's checking account. Also, jointly determine to what extent your child will be accountable for her or his expenditures and how and when your child will report all accountable expenditures to you.

Teenagers don't really like being financially dependent upon their parents; but in many cases, they have no choice. Realize that they may feel awkward or embarrassed by their need for money, as it is a sign that they are not as fully independent as they would like to be. With this in mind, do not withhold money as a bribe in order to pressure your daughter or son into living the way you think is best. You must still allow your child the freedom to make her or his own mistakes.

■ *Do not mistake homesickness as a sign of immaturity or an overly dependent adolescent.*

It is normal for a teenager to get homesick the first year away from home. You may get calls or letters about how much your child misses the family, favorite meals, or the room still waiting at home. The first attempts at living independently from the family create anxiety even in a well-balanced adolescent. Remember that your child's expressions of homesickness are probably not pleas to return home but merely signs that your child misses the friends, family members, routines, and environment to which she or he had grown accustomed. This is a natural feeling, and one that your child can—and should—manage on her or his own.

The "Return to the Nest" Syndrome

Shortly after leaving home to lead an independent life—either by going to college or taking a job—many adolescents will be compelled to return home again, at least for a while. This phenomenon is popularly known as the "return-to-the-nest" syndrome. Usually, it does not represent a failure or deficiency on the part of the returning children. Indeed, it's often a vital step toward successful growth. Maybe they couldn't work it out financially, a very difficult thing to do in today's economy, especially if they're simultaneously investing in their education or career advancement. Perhaps they were mature enough to realize that they felt too unsafe, too lonely, or too insecure to make a complete break from home just yet, and so they wisely decided it would be better to go through a "training period" of quasi-independence within the family domain.

Whatever the reason may be for your child's return to the nest, here are suggestions to make the new living arrangements more tolerable for all:

■ *Protect your own property and privacy.*
Your child is now an adult living in *your* home. It is no longer her or his home, and you have the right to determine how she or he occupies common rooms and intrudes on your own plans. While adult children living at home should not be treated like weekend guests, they should respect the fact that they are living in their parental home, not their own, and that their parents' plans and activities take precedence over theirs.

■ *Require your child to help around the house.*
A home-again teenager should not assume that she or he can live like a hotel guest and that her or his parents are the housekeeping staff. It is reasonable to expect everyone living in the house to pitch in with chores and maintenance tasks.

■ *Expect an adult child to contribute financially.*
Even if your daughter or son does not have a full-time job, she or he should contribute something to the household finances, even if it's only a token amount. If your child is employed and could be paying rent for an apartment, you have the right to expect a substantial monthly payment for room and board.

■ *Let adult children have their own personal lives.*
An adult child moving back home should not be expected to give up her or his private and personal life. You have the right to decide what type of behavior or activities you will allow in your home (such as no smoking or no overnight guests), but try to make every accommodation possible to let your child pursue the life she or he would be living if circumstances had not necessitated the move back home. Remember that what an adult child does *outside* your home does not fall under your jurisdiction, even if it is behavior of which you do not approve, such as drinking or premarital sex.

■ *Establish deadlines for moving out.*
Even though you and your child know that living at home will not be forever, it is wise to discuss the length of stay early after the child moves back in. Setting a deadline for when your adolescent will move back out gives her or him a target date to shoot for in terms of making career plans, saving money for rent, and finding a place to stay. When everyone accepts the current arrangement as temporary, it takes the edge off living together again when it becomes awkward or frustrating.

Programs to Expand Horizons

Many high schools are isolated from the worlds of work and politics, which await graduates like some remote lands they have only heard about in tales and legends. Some schools, however, have broken this isolation by developing contacts and networks within the business and political communities. Special career programs for high school students provide teenagers with the opportunity to work outside the school for academic credit or pay or both. But even more valuable, these programs help give teenagers more emotional maturity and a more responsible attitude toward their classroom studies.

Here are some programs you may want to investigate to help your daughter or son make career and vocational choices:

■ *Work-study* programs allow students to work for pay and receive academic credit for their experience. Some programs require the student to attend classes for part of the day and work outside the school for the remainder. The student gains valuable insights into the type of work she or he is doing, acquires information and skills that the job requires, and learns how to take supervision from professionals in the field.

■ *Human services* programs are designed to give students field experience in areas such as social work, the arts, law, education, and government agencies. They usually do not provide pay but often qualify for academic credit. Professional supervision teaches adolescents to follow orders, meet deadlines, and cooperate with others in an adult work environment.

■ *Vocational internships* are work programs that are part of vocational/technical course work at the school. Vocational internships benefit both companies and schools, in that they provide student workers for the company and hands-on experience for the students that cannot be offered on campus. Examples are carpentry students working for a building construction company or design students working for a fashion institute.

■ *Volunteer work* usually does not offer students pay or academic credit, but it provides valuable adult experiences outside the classroom. Many schools have ongoing volunteer programs with community agencies, such as daycare centers, environmental organizations, and urban recreational programs. Guidance counselors can advise your daughter or son on the type of volunteer work appropriate for her or his vocational goals.

11.

Psychotherapy

It's a common misconception that all teenagers are by nature a little bit crazy. Adolescence in general is assumed to be a time of great psychological turmoil, as opposed to the "happy" years of childhood and the "stable" years of adulthood. Thus, while some teenagers are considered more crazy than others, each one is regarded somewhat suspiciously, as if she or he were a risky experiment in living that might backfire at any moment, given the right—or, rather, wrong—circumstances.

Obviously, teenagers face psychological crises and pressures that are unique to their particular age group. Among the major ones are dealing with puberty and a newly emergent sexuality, planning and preparing for life after high school, breaking away from the world of the family, and assuming an increasingly independent personal and social identity. However, the early years of childhood, from birth to age six; the middle years of childhood, from age six to age thirteen; and the adult years, beginning around age twenty-one, each have their unique psychological crises and pressures as well.

The bottom line is that no one age group is basically "crazier" than another. To tag adolescence with the reputation of being an exceptionally trouble-ridden period of life is not only unjust; it is potentially harmful. Such a common value judgment predisposes many adolescents to be even more insecure about themselves than is warranted. It also encourages many parents to read psychological problems into their teenage child's behavior that in fact do *not* exist and—even more damaging—to dismiss psychological problems that *do* exist on the grounds that their child is no more disturbed than any other teenager is likely to be.

In determining whether or not to seek psychotherapeutic help for a teenage child, the challenge for parents is to distinguish between the *appearance* of emotional instability on the one hand and the *reality* of it on the other. This particular challenge is indeed more troublesome during a child's teenage years than it is during any other time in childhood.

If adolescence in general *appears* to be the most psychologically turbulent period of a child's life, it's largely a matter of the parents' built-in perspective. As a rule, parents tend to worry much more about the emotional welfare of their child during adolescence than they do during the years immediately preceding her or his adolescence.

There's no doubt that the potential consequences of an emotional disturbance during a child's adolescent years are much scarier for a parent to contemplate. Aside from the fact that adolescents are bigger, stronger, and more sexually developed than younger children and therefore more physically capable of inflicting violence upon themselves and others, adolescents are not nearly as responsive to parental control.

This loss of control is extremely difficult for any parent to handle with equanimity, even in the best of cases. Unfortunately, many parents unwittingly project their own emotional disturbance over their loss of control directly onto their teenage child, thereby making her or him appear to be the emotionally upset party instead of themselves.

In addition, parents can't help but feel that a psychological problem during a child's adolescent years poses a much more serious threat to her or his future success as an adult than one that occurs during the younger years. In other words, a preadolescent child is tacitly afforded more license to have emotional difficulties—whether they occur or not—than an adolescent child.

Admittedly, this is a shortsighted point of view. Unresolved psychological problems dating from early childhood are likely to have a far more entrenched and devastating effect on an adult's life than similar ones dating only from adolescence. However, it's understandable that parents are more and more inclined to worry about their child's future as that future looms closer and closer.

For example, parents are usually much more concerned about the negative effects that an emotional disturbance might have on their child's *high school* grades than they are about the negative effects that it might have on their child's *elementary school* performance. And parents are more apt to worry about society's opinion of their child's stealing, lying, or otherwise acting out psychological problems when she or he is a teenager than they are to worry about society's opinion of similarly motivated behaviors when she or he is only age seven, or nine, or eleven.

To make matters even more complicated, parents' memories of their own adolescence are generally more vivid, more extensive, and more emotionally charged than those of earlier childhood years. As a result, they have a greater ability to recall, imagine, and fear the emotional traumas that an adolescent might experience than those a younger child might face.

Here are some other "appearance-versus-reality" factors that can make it difficult for parents of an adolescent child to recognize if and when their child is experiencing serious psychological problems:

■ Adolescents spend a large percentage of time, day by day and week by week, away from their parents. Much of this separation is deliberately engineered: Adolescents crave the freedom to behave as they choose, without parental supervision. Thus, parents may not have sufficient exposure to their teenage child to detect that she or he is suffering emotional problems or, conversely, to appreciate that she or he is emotionally well adjusted and "normal" within her or his age range.

■ Adolescents are adept at "masking" their true state of mind. Instead of acting happy when they're happy, or sad when they're sad, they may display a neutral, "all purpose" demeanor that they maintain as often as possible—the classic "sullen" expression associated with adolescents. Or they may intentionally try to look annoyed when they're pleased, or content when they're troubled. These masking behaviors represent yet another extension of the typical teenager's intense desire for privacy. And they make it difficult for parents to determine how their teenage child truly feels.

■ Adolescents are often adamant about *not* letting their parents know that they're experiencing *any* problems, much less emotional problems. In some cases, the motivation is a desire not to appear incompetent or "babyish." In other cases, the motivation is more commendable, if equally self-centered: The teenager simply doesn't want to burden her or his parents with something that she or he personally finds so hard to bear.

■ Parents of adolescents are frequently unaware, or loath to admit, that they themselves are contributing to their child's emotional problems: for example, by being inappropriately overbearing, lenient, competitive, or distant. Thus, they literally don't see their child's emotional disturbances for what they really are. Instead, they perceive these problems more simplistically as "quirks" in their child's personality and behavior, "phases" in their child's progress through adolescence, or "attitudes" that their child is willfully and temporarily assuming for her or his own purposes.

Because so many factors can make it difficult for the parents of teenagers to determine whether or not their child is suffering from a serious emotional problem, they should be especially alert for the following most common indicators that a psychiatric evaluation might be useful:

■ a significant change for the worse in school performance;

■ evidence of prolonged substance abuse;

■ a consistent inability to cope with day-to-day activities and problems;

■ a dramatic change in sleeping or eating habits;

■ repeated complaints about physical ailments;

■ a persistent pattern of violating the rights of others;

■ a continual opposition to authority;

■ repeated incidents of illegal, illicit, or antisocial behavior (e.g., stealing, lying, truancy, vandalism);

■ a strong, irrational fear of becoming obese;

■ a persistent depression, characterized by negative mood, poor appetite, general passivity, and/or withdrawal;

■ a threat to commit suicide or a persistent, morbid interest in death or suicide;

■ repeated attempts to run away within a three-month period.

If you have any reason to believe that your teenage child's emotional health should be evaluated by a professional, don't hesitate to take action. The sooner you arrange for this evaluation, the better the chances are that you can catch any problems before they become even more serious. The evaluation itself may or may not reveal the need for actual psychotherapy.

As a rule, psychotherapeutic interventions involving adolescent children are relatively brief and pragmatic. Individual sessions typically last from forty-five minutes to two hours. In some cases, one or two sessions may be sufficient. For example, a concerned parent and child may just need professional reassurance that the child's psychological development is progressing normally or professional advice on strategies and activities that will foster more satisfying parent-child relations. In other cases, effective intervention may require weekly or biweekly sessions for several months or even hospitalization for anywhere from a few weeks to a year or more (although a year or more of hospitalization is very rare).

Specific goals for the psychotherapy of adolescent children generally include helping parents and child alike to interpret the latter's emotional state more accurately, increasing the quality and quantity of a child's—and a family's—social supports, and assisting all family members in coping with extrafamilial stressors in a more productive manner.

Case-by-case diagnostic techniques and treatments involving teen-age children vary considerably according to the specific situation and the actual age of the child. Generally, parental interviews are always a major part of the process. Parents are asked about their perceptions of their child, their relationship with their child, and their relationships with other family members, including their own parents.

Here are some issues to consider in finding the right doctor or therapist and the right type of therapy for you, your child, and your family:

1. Before you begin your search, establish what you consider is the problem that you want addressed and the goal that you want achieved.

First, write down your answers to the following five questions, bearing in mind that some of your answers may overlap:

a. What specific signs have I observed indicating that my child may be experiencing emotional turmoil? (As much as possible, give dates, times of day, settings, and circumstantial surroundings.)

b. How would I define this emotional turmoil? (In other words, if you had to make a diagnosis, what would it be?)

c. What might be the cause(s) of this turmoil? (Include any speculations you may have as well as any more conclusive opinions—being careful to distinguish between these two categories.)

d. In what different ways has this emotional turmoil been bothersome or detrimental to my child, to me, and to other members of the family? (Be as specific as possible, as you were directed to be in answering question a.)

e. How have I tried to better this situation? (Indicate which methods have been at least partially successful and which have failed altogether.)

Once you have answered all five questions to the best of your ability, write down a fairly succinct (one- or two-sentence) description of what you think the *problem* is. Next, write a similarly succinct description of the *goal* that you want to achieve related to this problem: that is, what you would like to see happen *as a result* of psychotherapeutic intervention.

These statements, as well as the question-and-answer background material, will be enormously helpful to you in interviewing possible doctors or therapists. They will also be enormously helpful to the doctor or therapist you choose in her or his efforts to diagnose and treat your child successfully.

2. *Familiarize yourself with the major types of therapy that are available.*

The sheer variety of therapy labels is bewildering to the outsider: psychoanalytic (Freudian, Jungian, Adlerian, or otherwise), cognitive, behavioral, existential, Gestalt, transactional, reality-oriented, rational-emotive, and so on. However, for the purpose of interviewing potential doctors or therapists to work with a teenage child, all you need is a very basic awareness of three broad categories of psychotherapy: psychodynamic therapy, behavioral therapy, and family-oriented therapy.

Let's consider each category individually:

■ *Psychodynamic therapy* is geared toward getting the child to identify, understand, and self-manage her or his emotional problems. It depends heavily on effective verbal communication between the doctor or therapist and the child. It also tends to be relatively long-term compared to the other categories of psychotherapy, often involving multiple sessions per week for up to a year or two.

■ *Behavioral therapy* is geared toward getting the child to change the way she or he behaves. Instead of focusing squarely on the causes of a particular problem, it concentrates on the symptoms. For example, it might help children learn to control their anger without necessarily getting them to appreciate why they get angry, to be less afraid of nightmares regardless of whether they know about their possible source, or to interact more cooperatively with other people even if their feelings about them remain unresolved. It typically takes at least a few months of weekly or biweekly sessions before satisfactory results can be expected.

■ *Family-oriented therapy*, sometimes known as "systems therapy," is the type of therapy practiced at Philadelphia Child Guidance Center (PCGC) and the type that PCGC recommends most highly for children of any age. Drawing upon both psychodynamic therapy and behavioral therapy, family-oriented therapy is geared toward generating positive awareness and change in all aspects of the child's world: her or his own mind and behavior as well as the minds and behaviors of those people who directly influence her or his life. The focus of the therapy is on interactions among family members and how these interactions influence each family member. In comparison to the other therapies, it is much more adaptable to the situation at hand. Satisfactory results may be achieved in just one or two sessions or may take up to a year or two to achieve.

Use these very basic distinctions as starting points for discussing with other people (such as knowledgeable advisers and potential doctors or therapists) the particular type or types of psychotherapy that may be appropriate for your unique situation. Investigate the literature about child psychotherapy that's available at local libraries and bookstores. The more informed you are about child psychotherapy—whatever form it may take—the more benefit you'll derive from the type you finally choose, whatever it may be.

3. Familiarize yourself with the major types of doctors and therapists that are available.

The three most common practitioners of child-oriented psychotherapy are psychiatrists, psychologists, and social workers. Regardless of the specific title (e.g., "child psychiatrist"), not all of these practitioners have special training or experience in treating children in particular, as opposed to people in general. This is an important issue that you will want to investigate with individual practitioners that you interview.

Also, keep in mind that one type of practitioner, all else being equal, is not necessarily more or less desirable than another type. Your final determination should be based on how appropriate the individual practitioner is, given the following factors: your child's problem, the goals you've established relating to that problem, the type of therapy you're interested in pursuing, your financial resources, and most important of all, the overall personalities of you and your child.

These warnings having been given, here are brief descriptions of each major type of practitioner:

■*Psychiatrists* are medical doctors (M.D.s), which means that they have had four years of medical school, one year of internship, and at least two years of residency training in psychiatry. In addition, virtually all child psychiatrists have had two-year fellowships in child psychiatry and are board certified.

One major advantage of a psychiatrist over other types of practitioners is that she or he can diagnose and prescribe treatment for physical problems that may be causing or aggravating a child's emotional problems. A possible disadvantage, depending on your particular situation, is that most psychiatrists are inclined to practice only psychodynamic forms of therapy.

■*Psychologists* have usually earned a doctorate (Ph.D.) in psychology, typically the result of five years of graduate training, including several supervised clinical programs and a year of formal internship. Most states also require postdoctoral experience before licensing. Some states, however, require only a master's degree (M.A.) to become a psychologist.

Although psychologists themselves cannot offer physical diagnosis and prescription, they almost always have close professional relationships with M.D.s whom they can recommend for such services. They are also likely to be more eclectic in their therapeutic style, although there is still a trend among psychologists to favor behavioral therapy.

■ *Social workers* have earned a master's degree in social work (M.S.W.), a process that involves two years of classes and fieldwork. In addition, some states require two or more years of postgraduate experience before licensing.

While social workers may not have had the extensive academic and clinical training that psychiatrists and psychologists have had, they are, as a rule, much more familiar with—and knowledgeable about—the home, community, and school environments of their clients. This background inclines them to practice family-oriented or systems-oriented therapy more than other types of therapy.

Another major issue to consider in choosing a particular type of doctor or therapist is whether the therapy will take place in a *private office* or in a *clinic*. Other factors aside, therapy performed in a clinic tends to be more multidimensional—a by-product of the fact that clinics are so often staffed with different types of doctors and therapists who not only practice different types of therapy but also conduct different kinds of research projects.

4. *Make a rough estimate of how much you can afford to spend on your child's therapy.*

It may be impossible to put a price on a child's emotional well-being. However, it's quite possible to determine how much you can afford to spend for psychotherapy without making life much more difficult for yourself and your family—a situation that could only exacerbate your child's emotional problems.

You may have insurance that will cover some or all of the expenses directly incurred as a result of your child's therapy; but in the best of situations there are bound to be some hidden costs. Factor into your budget such possibilities as lost income for days off work, transportation and parking for therapy sessions, and baby-sitting care for other children while you are at the sessions.

In estimating how much you can afford for the therapy itself, take into account that private therapy is almost certain to be more expensive than therapy in a clinic. Also, clinics may offer lower fees if you accept therapy from a supervised student therapist or agree to participate in a research project (which typically means being observed, taped, and/or interviewed).

5. Seek several recommendations from a variety of qualified sources.

Ask relatives and friends who have benefited from the services of child psychiatrists, psychologists, or social workers for their opinions, but also seek leads from more experienced and disinterested parties, such as your pediatrician, family physician, school counselor, and/or clergyperson. For the names of certified practitioners in your area, contact the local and national mental-health and professional organizations (see Appendix for a list of suggestions).

6. Interview different doctors and therapists thoroughly about their credentials, areas of expertise, and therapeutic techniques.

Among the specific questions you should ask are the following:

■ What is your educational and training background (see issue 3)?

■ Are you board certified? By whom?

■ With what professional organizations are you affiliated (see Appendix for a list)?

■ How long have you practiced in your current capacity?

■ What is your general or preferred style of therapy (see issue 2)?

■ What are your areas of special expertise?

■ How much work have you done with children who are the same age as my child?

■ How much work have you done with the type of problem(s) my child is having (see issue 1)?

■ Would you feel committed to achieving the goal I have in mind (see issue 1)?

■ What kinds of services can I expect from you toward meeting this goal?

■ What kinds of commitment and cooperation would you expect from me and my family in the course of my child's therapy?

■ How, and at what rate, will you keep me informed of the progress my child is making in therapy?

■ How much time do you estimate the therapy might take?

■ How much will it cost, will my insurance or medical assistance help pay the cost, and are there ways to reduce the cost (see issue 4)?

7. *Make sure that you choose a doctor or therapist who respects you and with whom you are comfortable.*
Some doctors or therapists may unintentionally cause you to feel guilty or incompetent, in which case you should look for someone else. The doctor or therapist you select should be a person who inspires you to feel good about yourself: *re*moralized, instead of *de*moralized.

Your answer to each of the following questions should be yes both during your initial interview with a doctor or therapist and for the time period that the therapy itself takes place.

■ Does the doctor or therapist take into account *your* theories, opinions, and concerns as well as her or his own?

■ Does the interaction you have with the doctor or therapist seem like a dialogue rather than a monologue on the doctor's or therapist's part?

■ Does the doctor or therapist seem genuinely interested in you and your situation (evidenced by paying close attention to you, maintaining fairly consistent eye contact with you, and regularly soliciting your comments and reactions)?

■ Does the doctor or therapist seem genuinely interested in your child and her or his problems?

■ Does the doctor or therapist take it upon her- or himself to make sure that you understand what she or he is doing and saying?

■ Does the doctor or therapist answer all your questions promptly, thoughtfully, and to the best of her or his ability?

■ Do you leave the doctor's or therapist's company feeling clear about the direction that your child's case will be taking?

■ Do you leave the doctor's or therapist's company feeling generally stronger rather than weaker?

Special Diagnoses: Adolescents

DEPRESSION

It used to be thought that so-called clinical depression was an adult psychiatric disorder. Over the past twenty years, it has increasingly been diagnosed among adolescents as well. Clinical depression for either an adult or an adolescent refers to a syndrome of multiple and severe depressive symptoms lasting for over three months (see pages 49–50 in this book for a list of adolescent depressive symptoms).

Psychotic features, such as hallucinations, obsessive thoughts, compulsive actions, or phobias, are often present in cases of clinical depression involving an adolescent, especially in extreme cases. But it is not *required* that such features be present to warrant a formal diagnosis. The same is true of suicidal thoughts or impulses toward self-destruction.

Typically, an episode of clinical depression in an adolescent is triggered by situational factors, for example, a poor adjustment to a new school, a major failure in peer relationships, a crisis in the family, or a severe dissatisfaction with one's performance or behavior. However, the serious nature of such a depression also suggests preexisting psychological and/or biochemical factors, which, if left untreated, are very likely to cause recurring and perhaps progressively worsening attacks of depression throughout the victim's life.

Successful psychotherapeutic treatment of a clinically depressed adolescent generally involves several months or more of individual and/or group sessions and sometimes one or more short periods of hospitalization (especially if the victim is suicidal). It may also involve antidepressant medication.

ANOREXIA NERVOSA

The most common psychiatric eating disorder afflicting teenagers, especially girls, is anorexia nervosa, or simply speaking, self-imposed starvation. Although the expressed purpose of a teenager's refusal to eat may be to lose weight or remain trim, the real motivation is a desperate need to experience a sense of mastery over life.

Typically, the anorexic teenager is a perfectionist who suffers from low self-esteem. This diminished self-esteem leads to an irrational self-image: The teenager persists in seeing her- or himself as too fat and too susceptible to self-indulgence regardless of how thin and self-denying she or he becomes.

Teenage girls are more subject to becoming victims of anorexia nervosa than teenage boys because of cultural factors. Not only do prevailing standards of beauty put far more pressure to be thin on women than on men, but also women are provided with fewer opportunities to feel that they have mastery over their lives.

In a relentless effort to avoid gaining weight (which, in itself, is a masked form of self-punishment), the anorexic teenager may actually starve her- or himself to the point where physical deterioration is irreversible, resulting in certain death if there is no medical intervention (and, in some cases, if medical intervention does not occur at a sufficiently early stage in the process). For this reason, it is vital to seek professional help for your child immediately if you have any reason to suspect anorexia.

BULIMIA

Bulimia is characterized by compulsively binging on huge quantities of high-calorie food and then purging oneself by self-induced vomiting or by using laxatives. The motivational pattern among teenage bulimics is similar to the pattern among teenage anorexics. Indeed, bulimic binges are often preceded or followed by periods of severe dieting.

Bulimia is much more widespread among female than male teenagers due to the same cultural differences that incline more women than men to become anorexic. Like anorexics, bulimics tend to be highly secretive about what they are going through. For example, a bulimic may hoard food or only binge during the middle of the night, while everyone else is asleep, or try to hide signs of throwing up by running water while spending long periods of time in the bathroom.

Among the possible negative effects of bulimia on the victim's physical health are severe dehydration, hormonal imbalance, and/or the depletion of important minerals. Fortunately, professional intervention at an early point stands an excellent chance of curing the victim of the compulsion toward bulimia.

Adolescence: Selected Terms and Concepts

acting out   indirectly expressing emotional conflicts—or "forbidden feelings"—through negative behavior. Such behavior is typically overdramatic and designed to attract attention. It may or may not be overtly self-punishing or injurious to others.

For example, a child who feels rejected by a parent may "act out" that feeling by refusing to speak to that parent, constantly trying to distract the parent, talking back, or picking fights with a sibling who appears to be getting more attention.

affective disorder   also known as *emotional disorder* or *mood disorder,* a specifically defined psychological illness relating to the emotions (e.g., *bipolar disorder*). Generally, such a disorder is apparent in the problematic manner in which a child physically displays her or his emotions (hence, the root "affect"). The disorder may also have a physical cause.

behavior modeling   a therapeutic technique by means of which the child is taught or encouraged to replace negative behaviors with more positive ones. The teaching or encouraging process involves modifying the way that each parent or caretaker interacts with the child so that the child learns by example or direct experience (e.g., a reward system) to behave more constructively.

bipolar disorder   also known as *manic-depressive disorder,* a psychological illness characterized by extreme mood swings back and forth between depression and elation. Each mood phase lasts for an indeterminant amount of time, varying from individual to individual and from episode to episode. The disorder has a biological basis and can often be controlled by medication.

cognitive disorder   a specifically defined mental problem relating to a child's perception, thought, learning, and/or memory processes. Such an illness generally has a biological cause and psychological effects.

A child may have suffered a particular cognitive disorder

from a very early age, or it may have developed over time. In either case, it is frequently not detected and diagnosed until adolescence, when a child's cognitive development is assumed to have reached maturity.

compliance   the tendency to respond effectively—both in emotional and behavioral terms—to scheduling arrangements, rules, and discipline.

conflict resolution   a therapeutic technique in which a child is assisted in alleviating or managing chronic interpersonal conflict. Often group therapy is involved, bringing together the child with the other person or persons involved in the conflict. The therapy may also, or alternatively, feature one-on-one teaching, whereby the child learns general strategies for handling interpersonal conflicts more effectively.

defense mechanism   according to Sigmund Freud's terminology, a means unconsciously and automatically employed by the psyche to avoid emotional pain, such as *denial*, *projection*, or *repression*.

delinquency   also known as *juvenile delinquency,* a legal term applied to the antisocial, immoral, or transgressive behavior of minors (who, in most states, are children under eighteen years old). Manifested by an adult, the same behavior would most likely be construed as criminal and therefore legally liable.

In psychological terms, such behavior in a child is often motivated by emotional problems relating to adjustment, identity, or conduct. However, the behavior may also be partly or entirely motivated by social, economic, cultural, or "life-style" forces (e.g., peer pressure, discrimination, poverty, substance abuse).

denial   a conscious or unconscious refusal to acknowledge or accept unpleasant thoughts or situations. An automatic, self-protective measure, denial is particularly apparent among adolescents because of their heightened self-awareness and expanded social horizons.

depression   more technically known as *unipolar disorder*, a term that refers to a distinct psychological illness characterized by chronic apathy, hopelessness, and fatigue—physical as well as emotional.

dysfunctional   as opposed to *functional*, a term used to describe a personality or family unit that does not operate effectively or satisfactorily to meet day-to-day life challenges. In some cases, there is apparent effectiveness or satisfaction, but achieving it causes underlying psychological damage. In other cases, the personality or family unit is clearly having problems that pose a threat to its survival.

This term is sociological in origin and is rapidly losing currency in the field of psychology. Many therapists consider it too negative and abstract to be useful diagnostically.

emotional disorder   (see *affective disorder*)

functional   (see *dysfunctional*)

juvenile delinquency   (see *delinquency*)

maladaptation   also known as *maladjustment*, this term refers to a child's inability to respond in a calm, effective, or successful manner either to a single life change or to the demands of life in general.

maladjustment   (see *maladaptation*)

manic-depressive disorder   (see *bipolar disorder*)

medical intervention   in most cases, the use of medication (e.g., tranquilizing drugs) to alleviate the cause or symptoms of a psychological problem.

mood disorder   (see *affective disorder*)

neurosis   as opposed to the more serious condition *psychosis*, a psychological problem that still allows the victim to maintain reasonably good contact with reality and perform intellectually in a reasonably acceptable manner.

This term does not refer to a specific illness. Therefore, it is technically not accurate to say that a child is suffering from a *neurosis*. Because of this fact, the term is rapidly being replaced by the expression "neurotic process" (e.g., "If treatment is not applied, this child's emotional problem could trigger a neurotic process").

obsessive-compulsive disorder   a psychological problem characterized by intense, highly disruptive preoccupation with performing a certain ritualized activity. This activity may or may not be related to "normal life" tasks. For example, one person suffering from obsessive-compulsive disorder may be fanatically neat in her or his personal grooming (a "normal life" task); another person suffering from the disorder may be driven to scrub her or his bedroom walls every week (not a "normal life" task).

Such a disorder generally does not manifest itself in an individual's life prior to adolescence. However, early signs that such a disorder may be developing can occur during a child's middle years, in behaviors that are indeed obsessive but far less disruptive to the child and those around her or him (e.g., frequent and ritualized hand washing).

overcorrection   a negative effect of the parent-child relationship in which the discipline or punishment imposed on a child's conduct—or the child's "reforming" response to discipline or punishment—exceeds appropriate limits.

pathology   (see *psychopathology*)

personality disorder   a psychological problem relating to acquired and entrenched character traits or patterns of personal behavior that are injurious to the child or to others. Generally, the child does not realize such traits or behaviors are problematic, but those who are in contact with the child easily and quickly do.

projection   an unconscious, self-protecting measure in which a child denies her or his own negative, forbidden, or unpleasant feelings and instead attributes them to someone else. In most cases, the person upon whom the child projects such feelings is the trigger for them. For example, a child who is angry at Mother may unconsciously reclaim her or his innocence by believing instead that Mother is angry with her or him.

psychoanalysis   as opposed to the broader term *psychotherapy*, a mode of diagnosing and treating a child's psychological problems through one-on-one patient-therapist dialogue. There are many different schools of psychoanalysis, each based on a particular philosophy regarding how the psyche functions.

psychopathology   the study of mental illnesses. The term *pathology* refers to a disease or disorder, as opposed to a less severe problem.

psychosis   as opposed to the less serious condition *neurosis*, a psychological problem that often or continuously prevents the victim from maintaining reasonably good contact with reality or from performing intellectually and socially in a reasonably acceptable manner.

A particular psychotic disorder may be psychological in origin, biological in origin, or both. Among the distinctive indicators that an emotional problem is psychotic rather than neurotic are the presence of delusions (irrational beliefs) or hallucinations (distorted perceptions).

psychotherapy a professional method of treating emotional problems and *affective disorders*. Psychotherapy can take a number of different forms, such as *psychoanalysis*, or varying therapies designed to provide appropriate *behavior modeling*.

repression a means of emotional self-protection in which traumatic or unpleasant thoughts or memories are automatically relegated to the unconscious mind and forgotten by the conscious mind.

resilience a child's ability to adapt effectively to change or recover effectively from a crisis. The more resilient a child's emotional nature is, the psychologically healthier she or he is.

resistance in the context of psychotherapy, a child's conscious or unconscious refusal to cooperate with the therapist or the therapy.

suicidal ideation a child's thoughts or verbal expressions having to do with suicide. Some verbal expressions may be direct (e.g., the statement "I feel like killing myself"); others may be indirect (e.g., "Life just doesn't seem worth living"). For safety's sake, expressions of either type should always be regarded as possible indicators of serious suicidal intention. (For more information, see the "Depression" section, especially "Preventing Teenage Suicide.")

unipolar disorder (see *depression*)

withdrawal a child's willful separation, emotional and/or physical, from an event or person that is somehow distressing. Long-term withdrawal, or an ever-widening pattern of withdrawal, can be a sign of an underlying psychological problem.

Appendix

Organizations to Contact

If you believe your child is having serious problems dealing with her or his emotions or behavior, it's a good idea to get a professional evaluation of your child's emotional health and, possibly, professional help for your child. These services should be provided by a well-qualified child psychiatrist, child psychologist, or social worker whom both you and your child like and trust.

To find the professional that's right for your situation, first consult friends and relatives who have had experience with such services, your pediatrician, and your child's school counselor. Also try local organizations, such as medical societies, psychiatric societies, and city, county, and state mental-health associations.

If you are unable to get satisfactory references or locate an acceptable professional using these sources, or if you'd like more background information on the subject and practice of psychotherapy for children, try contacting any of the following organizations for assistance:

American Academy of Child and Adolescent Psychiatry
3615 Wisconsin Avenue, NW
Washington, DC 20016
(800) 222-7636

■ professional society for degreed physicians who have completed an additional five years of residency in child and adolescent psychiatry

■ forty-three regional groups in the United States, equipped to provide information (including consumer guidance on insurance benefits covering child and adolescent psychiatry) and referrals

American Academy of Community Psychiatrists
P.O. Box 5372
Arlington, VA 22205
(703) 237-0823

■ professional society for psychiatrists and psychiatry residents practicing in community mental-health centers or similar programs that provide care regardless of their client's ability to pay

■ seven regional groups in the United States that are equipped to inform the public about a community psychiatrist's training and role and about how to obtain services

American Association of Psychiatric Services for Children
1200-C Scottsville Road, Suite 225
Rochester, NY 14624
(716) 235-6910

■ accrediting service and information clearinghouse for clinics and other institutions offering psychiatric services for children

■ equipped to provide information and referrals

National Association of Social Workers
7981 Eastern Avenue
Silver Spring, MD 20910
(800) 638-8799

■ professional society for people who hold a minimum of a baccalaureate degree in social work (B.S.W.)

■ fifty-five state, district, and protectorate groups that are equipped to inform the public about the services provided by social workers and how to obtain them

American Association for Marriage and Family Therapy
1717 K Street, NW #407
Washington, DC 20006
(202) 429-1825

■ professional society for marriage and family therapists

■ maintains thirty-nine training centers throughout United States that are equipped to provide information and referrals

Psychology Society
100 Beekman Street
New York, NY 10038
(212) 285-1872

■ professional society for psychologists who have a doctorate and are certified/licensed in the state where they practice

■ equipped to provide information and referrals

National Association for the Advancement of Psychoanalysis
and the American Boards for Accreditation and Certification
80 Eighth Avenue, Suite 1210
New York, NY 10011
(212) 741-0515

■ professional society for psychoanalysts that sets standards for training, accredits institutions, certifies individual practitioners, and evaluates institutions and practitioners

■ equipped to offer information and referrals (publishes an annual directory, *National Registry of Psychoanalysts*, with geographic index: $15)

*Council for the National Register of Health Service Providers
in Psychology*
1730 Rhode Island Avenue, NW, Suite 1200
Washington, DC 20036
(202) 833-2377

■ registry for psychologists who are licensed or certified by a state board of examiners of psychology and who have met additional council criteria as health service providers in psychology

■ equipped to provide referrals

National Council of Community Mental Health Centers
12300 Twinbrook Parkway
Rockville, MD 20852

■ membership organization of community mental-health centers

■ not equipped to provide referrals by telephone but publishes a bi-annual *National Registry*, which lists centers by geographic area

Federation of Families for Children's Mental Health
1021 Prince Street
Alexandria, VA 22314
(703) 684-7710

■ organization for parents looking for support and advocacy groups

■ equipped to provide contacts

Index